The
All American
War Game

For Linda

The
All American
War Game

JAMES LAWTON

Basil Blackwell

First published 1984
Reprinted 1984

Basil Blackwell Publisher Limited
108 Cowley Road, Oxford OX4 1JF, England

British Library Cataloguing in Publication Data

Lawton, James
    The all American war game.
    1. Football
    I. Title
    796.332 GV940

ISBN 0–631–13473–5

Typeset by Katerprint Co Ltd, Oxford
Printed in Great Britain by Billings and Son Ltd, Worcester

Contents

Illustrations

Diagrams of play appear between pages 44 and 45. A plate section appears between pages 52 and 53.

Acknowledgements

My thanks go to Pat Hickey, who prepared the glossaries and gave much valuable advice. Also most generous with their time and knowledge were Archie McDonald, Jim Kearney, Jim Taylor and Tom Larscheid. This book could not have been written without the kindness and patience of many American and Canadian players and writers. My gratitude and respect go to them all. I am also most grateful to Kiff Holland for drawing the diagrams.

Plates 10, 11, 12, 13, 18, 19, 20, 21, and 23 are reproduced by courtesy of the Pro Football Hall of Fame in Canton, Ohio, and plates 1, 2, 3, 4, 5, 6, 7, 8, 9, 14, 15, 16, 17, 22, 24, 25, and 26 by courtesy of National Football League Properties, Inc., Los Angeles.

Introduction

American football is about many things. It is about great skill and brute power, about American tradition and ambition and, in a real sense, the way the world's richest, most self-indulgent society sees itself. Most of all, American football is about money.

At the apex of this wealth is the National Football League (NFL). There are twenty-eight clubs split into two conferences, the National Football Conference and the American Football Conference. Each conference is divided into three divisions along loose geographic lines. The breakdown is as follows:

NATIONAL FOOTBALL CONFERENCE: East Division—Dallas Cowboys, Washington Redskins, New York Giants, St Louis Cardinals and Philadelphia Eagles; Central Division—Tampa Bay Buccaneers, Minnesota Vikings, Green Bay Packers, Detroit Lions and Chicago Bears; West Division—Atlanta Falcons, San Francisco 49ers, Los Angeles Rams and New Orleans Saints.

AMERICAN FOOTBALL CONFERENCE: East Division—New York Jets, Miami Dolphins, Buffalo Bills, New England Patriots and Baltimore Colts; Central Division—Cincinnati Bengals, Pittsburgh Steelers, Cleveland Browns and Houston Oilers; West Division—San Diego Chargers, Los Angeles Raiders, Seattle Seahawks, Kansas City Chiefs and Denver Broncos.

Each club plays sixteen regular season games. The six conference winners automatically go forward to the play-offs for the Super Bowl. In addition there are four "wild card" qualifiers comprising the two teams from each conference with the best records who failed to win their divisions.

The NFL is a triumph for both the ruthless American business ethic . . . and pragmatism. The League is superbly marketed, and so anxious are the authorities for games to be close, enthralling duels that each year the fixture list is adjusted. Successful teams will find their list of opponents dominated by powerful or improving clubs; losers will be largely bracketed with fellow strugglers or teams demonstrably on the slide. The result is generally a program of tense, evenly fought fixtures, crucial for the manipulation of drama on television.

Television and gambling are the two other crucial elements in the extraordinary success of the League, in the greening of football. I live in the Canadian city of Vancouver, which is just a half-hour's drive from the US border. At a cost of $14 per month I am hooked into cable television and have a choice of some fourteen channels. The result is that each weekend during the football season there is an extraordinary range of live action at my disposal. Here is an example of a typical weekend in September 1983. Saturday a.m., University of Illinois versus Michigan State; Saturday p.m., Iowa versus Ohio State University, Notre Dame versus University of Miami. In addition, on Canadian channels there are live games from Toronto and Winnipeg. Sunday a.m., Pittsburgh Steelers versus New England Patriots; Sunday p.m., Washington Redskins versus Seattle Seahawks, St Louis versus Philadelphia. Monday p.m., New York Giants versus Green Bay Packers. All this represents twenty-seven hours of live football. If I chose to abandon family life totally, I could pay a few dollars more for a private cable service that would supply me with twenty-four hours of continuous sport, much of it recorded and much of it football.

Staggeringly, most of these games, certainly the American ones, are played before sell-out crowds in huge stadiums. Live television, presented with superb technical accomplishment, has proved a great stimulus for live audiences. Games are not transmitted locally unless the home club or university has sold all its tickets.

Before each game transmission there is a lingering aerial shot of the ground and its environs. This is not designed simply for dramatic effect. It is a service for gamblers who, it has been estimated, wager more than $1 billion on college and NFL football each weekend. If there are clear skies above Cincinnati and San Diego are the visitors, gamblers will have a clear inkling of the way the game will go. Dry weather means that San Diego's passing game will not be hindered by a slippery ball. If it is wet, Cincinnati's powerful ground game will have more effect. Either way it may be that gamblers will look more carefully at the "spread." The spread is the handicapping system devised by bookmakers. Betters are invited not simply to pick a winner but to gauge the margin of victory. Their team may lose, but if they are within a few points of powerful opposition, the wager may be good. It is another device to heighten interest in games that might otherwise be mundane.

There is much to fascinate in the more sporting aspects of gridiron football, in the character of the players and the tactics of the coaching, but any understanding of it as a phenomenon has to be informed by the fact that without television and gambling it would today probably be just another game. As it is, American football is the richest game of all.

1

Bombs Away!

Terry Bradshaw, quarterback of the Steelers, steps back from the line of scrimmage. His right arm is already cocked as he peers downfield, squinting a little in the winter sunshine. Bradshaw, a blonde, laconic man from the bayou country of Louisiana, is waiting for his moment, even as a huge opponent—6 feet 8 inches tall and weighing 277 pounds—lunges towards him. Bradshaw's assailant has penetrated a wall of black-and-gold uniformed players, whose task is to throw up a protective screen and whose job effectiveness can generally be gauged by the health of the quarterback at season's end.

In the great stands there is an atavistic sound. It wells in thousands of throats and is not unlike the one you hear at the Plaza de Toros when the crowd sees that the matador is in trouble. Here in Pittsburgh's gaunt Three Rivers Stadium the perception is that Bradshaw will be sacked. The sack is the triumph of the dark force of the defensive unit. The sack is when a quarterback is hurled to the ground, when the most glamorous figure in football in stripped of his glory and his pretensions. One of the most famous of current marauders, Mark Gastineau of the New York Jets, has taken to performing a victory dance over the fallen quarterback. Some believe this is in the poorest of taste, that to gloat publicly over a fallen opponent is somehow deeply at odds with the ethos of football. Football, they argue, should be played by young men in tune with the spirit of the old values, of fortitude, courage and an awareness of individual dignity. Gastineau says that he is merely expressing emotions which have been felt as long as the game has been played, and there is no doubt that a large section of the crowd that gathers in Shea Stadium, New York, considers a sack by Gastineau and his reaction to it the emotional centerpiece of the game.

But such a celebration would be premature here in Pittsburgh. Bradshaw is a master of timing. Indeed, he is the kind of man you would want in the foxhole, chewing gum, weighing options and giving no hint of fear.

What may be trouble for another quarterback is often

opportunity for Bradshaw, and in these few seconds the truly perceptive may have noted that his gaze downfield has not been broken by the fury around him, the urgent roar of the crowd and the pounding feet of the man who wants to sack him and who is already making strange gurgling sounds of anticipation. Downfield, a receiver has broken free of his coverage and, like the shutter of a camera, Bradshaw freezes the moment. He releases the ball in a huge, looping trajectory. The receiver is in the end zone, climbing high to pull down the ball. He rolls on the astroturf, the ball safe in his grasp. Nothing in football can match the beauty of such a move, and it is no surprise to learn that the Pittsburgh receiver, Lynn Swann, a lean, handsome black man from California, spends much of his time in a ballet studio. Yet even when football soars away from the trenches, even when it is at its most delicate, the language of the game remains uncompromising. What Bradshaw has achieved, in the idiom of this language, is the throwing of a perfect bomb.

American football has always been considered intrinsically and obscurely American by the rest of the world. New devotees abroad have listed many reasons for their attraction. They have talked about American football's explosive action. They have dwelt on the speed and the artistry and timing exemplified by the combination of a Bradshaw and a Swann. They have discussed a sense of excitement, of color, of engagement. This is fine as far as it goes, but it perhaps misses the essential point about American football. It is an activity that observes many of the conventions of sport, but always the game has a meaning and a psychology that can never be contained within the parameters of the field. This, of course, can be true of other sports, but in American football the point is insistent. If all of sport is a magnificent triviality, American football seems least tolerant of the limitation.

Just as Ernest Hemingway warned his fellow Americans that they should abandon their own sense of morality when they attend their first bullfight, it seems reasonable to suggest to non-Americans that what happens on the gridirons of American cities and colleges and high schools is as much ritual as sport, as much a test of manhood as of skill. American football, quintessentially, is about war.

Marshal Foch, fresh from the battlefields of Picardy, grasped the point immediately when he attended his first game. He was taken to the annual Army–Navy game in Philadelphia in 1919, and before the end of the first quarter he exclaimed to his companion, an American general, "*Mon Dieu*, this game is war! It has everything." Indeed it has. It has everything to thrill a military mind. It has the trench warfare of the behemoths who crouch on the line of scrimmage, growling and cussing like infantrymen, hoping to win a little ground, a little time. It has the outriders, the receivers, ghosting through lines of defense. It has the running backs, who operate as armor, punching holes in the cover, testing, probing, looking for a point of breakthrough. By the time Marshal Foch saw his first game the forward pass had been legalized, so the paratroop brigades were already forming; soon there would also be strikes from the air.

You think the metaphor of war is stretched? The suspicion would not last long in the company of football coaches or even that of many players. It was said of one college coach, Pappy Waldorf of the University of California, Berkeley, "He could make one game seem like the Punic Wars." Waldorf's prime was in the 1950s and 1960s, when he was a legend in the bars and bistros in the hills overlooking the Bay of San Francisco, but his kind of imagery has scarcely softened in the 1980s.

Pittsburgh's Bradshaw was recently asked for his assessment of the San Diego Chargers, a team with striking offensive potential but notoriously weak in defense. Bradshaw concluded, correctly, that San Diego's defensive frailty would deny them a triumph in the Super Bowl, but he added, "I'll tell you this, if America gets in another war, I'll send San Diego out to run the offense. Air power, bombs, those big tanks on the line. Who'd stop them?"

That football was a suitable motif for American power was made clear enough by the Pentagon in 1942. Two American football games were played between US and Canadian servicemen in London's Wembley Stadium that year. The first game was called the Tea Bowl in deference to the somewhat bemused English hosts. Much to the horror of the Pentagon, the Canadians perpetrated a massacre. The Canadians, a little further into the war effort in Europe, had on hand several leading professional players from the Canadian Football League. Jeff Nicklin, a tight end for the Winnipeg Blue Bombers, was particularly rampant, throwing ferocious blocks and finding wide-open spaces. He made several touchdowns. Though the

Allies were merely hanging on to North Africa at the time, though the Japanese were virtually at the gates of Sydney Harbor, it seemed that the fate of the American team at Wembley was a top priority at the Pentagon. There is a report, perhaps apocryphal, that an American running back was plucked from the jungles of Guadalcanal and flown to England. What is certain is that the US team that showed up for the hastily arranged second game bore no resemblance to the one that had been so ill-treated by the Canadians.

THE FLYING WEDGE: A TRYST WITH DEATH

The second game was called the Coffee Bowl. It had a more familiar, more reassuring, ring perhaps. The Americans won their Coffee Bowl handily. And later, with a sad kind of symmetry, the former Blue Bomber Nicklin, who had done so much to win the first aerial battle of Wembley, died in his parachute over Normandy.

In 1952 American football returned to Wembley. There was a game between the winners of US service tournaments in West Germany and Britain. A crowd of 30,000 braved a bleak November afternoon. By half-time the gathering had shrunk to a smattering of drill sergeants, potential GI brides and a few dogged natives determined to establish some meaning, any meaning, to a game that had been turned into one of life's ultimate mysteries by a tactic, then briefly in vogue, known as the Split-T formation. The Split-T put great emphasis on the running game. There was much "faking" in the backfield, which is to say one running back would suggest he had the ball and make a decoy move, while another would drive off in an entirely different direction. This meant that few players and even fewer spectators actually caught a glimpse of the ball.

But if the Split-T was a passing aberration that brought confusion to casual spectators on a foreign field, it was the purest of sunlight when compared with an earlier tactic, the Flying Wedge. The Split-T merely killed the game as a spectacle. The Flying Wedge literally killed the football players. Eighteen players were said to have died as a direct result of the tactic in 1905. The statistic is less startling when you know that the Flying Wedge required players to charge in a V-shaped phalanx, the ball carrier theoretically protected by a "wedge" of blockers but ultimately used as a human battering ram. The point of the exercise, of course, was to get the ball over the line, and the feeling was that this could be done most efficiently if it was wrapped in a human being. There was a cost—pain and broken limbs and sometimes life itself—but such was the price of glory on the football field, as on the battleground. To keep the wedge intact suitcase handles were stitched into the players' uniforms. The idea was to grab hold of the handles and maintain a grasp until a touchdown was scored or death intervened. In 1906 President Theodore Roosevelt, reviewing casualty figures from the previous winter, decided that eighteen such interventions were way too many. He summoned the game's organizers to Washington. He said the Flying Wedge had to go. It was incompatible with a civilized society. Glum and wounded, the football administrators decided that rather than see the game abolished, they would banish the Flying Wedge. Any fears that the game would become effete were proved groundless quickly enough, however.

Deaths and serious injury still occur regularly in high school and college football, and psychologists say that for every physical mishap there are many more stories of scarring of the spirit. Dr Thomas Tutko of San José State University cites the case that he considers a classic. It involves a prodigious young football player who won every honor at high school and university and was drafted by the most prestigious of professional clubs, Dallas Cowboys of the National Football League. Dallas, apart from having the world's most beautiful cheerleaders, have the unofficial title of "America's Team." When the young football player was being interviewed by Dallas officials he broke down in tears, first to the disbelief, then to the horror of his interlocutors. He said that he had never enjoyed football and he just could not go through with a professional career. He had played the game to please his parents, his teachers, his friends. Everyone expected him to play; everyone attached great value to what he did on the field. For half his life he had been playing a part, fulfilling other people's dreams. His life had become a misery, an existence dominated by the imperatives of football, by the instructions barked down a bullhorn by coaches for whom the game was an end in itself. He was sorry, but he had to walk away and try to forget football. Tutko argues that Vince

Lombardi, the great coach of Green Bay Packers, did untold damage to the mental health of generations of Americans when he made his famous declaration: "Winning isn't everything. It is the only thing." The tear-stained young man in Dallas was merely an example of someone who had dared to step out of the football closet.

On an evening in January 1983, in the bar of the large Los Angeles hotel that was official headquarters for the XVII National Football League Super Bowl—the Roman numerals are just one small example of the game's obsession with creating instant history—I fell into casual conversation with an immaculately dressed black businessman. Inevitably, the talk turned to the approaching game between the Washington Redskins and the Miami Dolphins and then meandered in other directions. I expressed my surprise that soccer had never taken serious hold professionally on the continent, especially in cities like Los Angeles and New York, with their large Latin populations. I said that until quite recently it had seemed inevitable that the world game would conquer its last frontier.

"Never in a thousand years," declared the businessman. "Anyone who understands America will tell you that football will always be the American game. Football is the perfect expression of American life. Its demarcation lines are very clear. Hell, they even draw lines across the field, marking off the yardage. The game is like American life. If you do well, you are rewarded, you win ground. If you do badly, make a mistake, you have to pay, step back in the line. Soccer is not like this at all. In soccer a guy can run around for ninety minutes without appearing to do anything. Then suddenly he can score a goal and he is a hero. We cannot understand a game like that. We have to have impact, and action, and instant reward, and punishment. Soccer is too subtle for most Americans. I'm afraid it's as simple as that."

Though he lived locally, the businessman was not going to Pasadena's Rose Bowl for the big game. "I will watch it with my two sons at home. We will spend the day in the den sitting in front of the television, watching the pre-game show, analyzing the teams, reading statistics. Nothing will interfere." It has been said that if the Russians ever invade North America, they would be wise to choose the last Sunday in January, Super Bowl day. Almost the entire population will be watching the

game. For thirty seconds of commercial air time on the Super
Bowl telecast the cost is $300,000. It is as though the most
powerful nation on earth sits down for a day and reacquaints
itself with its most basic values. What the American people saw
at Pasadena on the last Sunday of January in 1983 was a
restatement of those values in the very bluntest of terms.

John Riggins, fullback of the Washington Redskins, made the
statement, wordlessly. He destroyed the Miami Dolphins in the
most elemental of ways. He simply overwhelmed them physically. He had said to his coach, the quiet, God-fearing Joe Gibbs,
"Give me the ball and I'll do the rest."

A week earlier the 33-year-old Riggins had intimated strongly
that he was a man of destiny. He had run for a total of 140 yards
against the formidable Dallas Cowboys in the National Football
Conference Final at Washington's RFK Stadium. Running 140
yards may seem a modest achievement, especially to a soccer
player. For a running back 140 yards is a rich yield indeed. The
ground has to be won against some of the biggest and fastest
athletes in the world of professional sport; it has to be snatched
from the barest patches of daylight as your blockers thud against
linemen and linebackers. There is no respite in the matter of
gaining 140 yards against a team like the Dallas Cowboys,
though when Riggins came to Pasadena America was still
skeptical about both him and his team.

The victory over Dallas earned Washington their place in the
Super Bowl—Miami's defense had proved too good for the New
York Jets in the American Football Conference final—but there
were suspicions that the empire of Dallas coach Tom Landry
had begun to fray. Ralph Wiley of *Sports Illustrated*, the magazine
which each week tells Americans all they ever wanted to know
about football and sometimes more, wrote of the game: "Across
the fifty states, last Saturday will live as the day America's Team
was exposed for what it had become, a creaking battleship that
had seen its best days, its engines straining, the rifling in its gun
barrels worn out. On a chill, overcast afternoon Washington
Redskins beat Dallas Cowboys, roundly, soundly, as if they were
Anybody's Old Team. The Republic may never be the same."

ON THE DAY OF THE DOLPHINS, AN EXPLOSIVE PACKAGE

In Pasadena Riggins restored the Republic's morale. He was, as it happened, an unlikely football hero despite his superb physique (6 feet 2 inches, 230 pounds). There had been times when his reclusive leanings and eccentric style hinted at disdain for the rigid codes of football. Once he painted his toenails green before he went to play. His haircut had ranged from full Afro to Mohawk. When he was drafted to the New York Jets, as a graduate of the University of Kansas, he was asked if it was the most exciting day of his life. He said, no, that day had occurred back in Kansas, "watching my neighbor's pigs being born." After he moved from New York to Washington he did little to change his rebellious image. Once he walked out of pre-season training camp in an attempt to bolster his contract. He said, drily, "I went fishing but they weren't biting." Despite his formidable work on Washington's approach to the Super Bowl, there was still something skittish, almost fey, about his attitude in the days before the big game.

At one of the bizarre pre-game press conferences, where as many as 100 writers and radio reporters attempt to conduct separate interviews with the same player in a great tangle of TV cables, Riggins was asked whether he was worried about the burden of expectation he carried to Pasadena. Riggins replied, "I was camping out one night with an old fella named Glenn Jenkins back in Centralia, Kansas, and I could hear the coyotes howling, and they sounded like they were getting mighty close. I asked Glenn if he felt nervous and he said, 'I've probably killed 200 of them. It doesn't exactly raise the hair on the back of my neck. It's like NFL games. I've probably gone through 130 of them and they don't exactly raise the hair on the back of my neck.'"

By the end of Super Bowl XVII the hairs on the back of Miami necks snapped to attention whenever the ball was handed to John Riggins. Washington's coach Gibbs, who had learned his business under the guidance of San Diego's brilliant offensive strategist Don Coryell, had worked to deflect Miami from the central threat of Riggins's running power. Among his devices was something called the Explode Package. This involved the team's five possible receivers moving in strange patterns before the "snap" of the ball from center to quarterback at the line of scrimmage. It was the most blatant of diversionary moves, and it did not fool Miami for long. Coached by Don Shula, one of the NFL's most respected tacticians, Miami identified Riggins as their main problem from start to finish. But identifying the problem was one thing. Dealing with it effectively was another.

For a time Shula's Dolphins achieved a kind of parity. The fine linebacker A. J. Duhe, a hero of the triumph over New York, was no less versatile in this game as Miami sought to contain Riggins, limit the damage as he built steam behind a blocking team which called themselves, proudly, the Hogs. But Hog power had it in the end. Riggins became unplayable as Hogs such as Joe Jacoby (277 pounds) cleared chinks of space. Jacoby said that he could see that the Dolphins were tiring. "I could see by their breathing how tired they were, the way their chests were heaving and the steam was coming off them."

Breaking point came in the fourth quarter. Riggins, his path carved by a small running back-blocker named Otis Wonsley and tight end Clint Didier, swept around the left end of the line. He was carrying the ball for the thirtieth time in the game. He ran 43 yards for a touchdown. The Day of the Dolphins was over.

President Ronald Reagan called coach Gibbs and talked of his admiration for "Rigginomics." "If only Reaganomics would work so well," sighed the President. Reaganomics and its "trickle-down" economics was subtle, not easily grasped by a blue-collar worker in Detroit or Milwaukee, who knew only that his paycheck or welfare payment seemed a little more inadequate each week. Reaganomics depended on so many factors—world markets, interest rates, investor confidence. Rigginomics was beautifully simple. Rigginomics was about giving a man the ball and letting him run. Rigginomics was about the old kind of American power.

Washington's coach Gibbs thanked the President for his call and then thanked God, several times. For a few hours a whole continent seemed to be at peace with itself.

In fact, the 1983 Super Bowl was an extraordinary triumph for the game, one that could not have been predicted just a few months earlier. Then football seemed to be as ravaged by the times as any other branch of national life.

First of all, there was the unthinkable. There was talk of a strike of football players. Hints of Marxism had turned into such grim realities as the sight of opponents shaking hands with each other—as a mark of "solidarity"—in pre-season exhibition games. The fans booed and the owners of the twenty-eight National Football League clubs—the richest professional sports league in the world—closed ranks. The players, led by lawyer Ed Garvey, were asking for 55 per cent of the gross earnings of the league. They produced formidable statistics. They pointed out that the career life of a football player was 4.2 years, that the cost of a professional career was usually severe physical pain for the rest of life. Knees were usually the first to go. "The knee joint isn't built for football," said one doctor, "and this is especially so on artificial turf." The football players pointed to the skyrocketing wages of baseball and basketball players in leagues that made only a fraction of the profits of football. The owners, through their suave spokesman Jack Donlan, suggested they were being hit by communism.

Certainly, there were some fine ironies. One management sympathizer pointed out that a leading players' activist had taken along a baseball bat in an attempt to break a strike of waiters at a restaurant in which he had interests. A collision was inevitable, and it happened three games into the regular season.

The players walked off the job, and for weeks it seemed that the season would die. Garvey waged a poor attack on the establishment. His arguments for profit-sharing and his emphasis on reward for long service failed to strike many chords, either with leading players or with the general public. There were defectors, important ones, including Pittsburgh's Bradshaw. America was having a hard time in the factories and out on Main Street. The football players had misread the times. Finally, the players accepted a deal that didn't come close to their original demands, and Garvey was a spent force in football. Months after the débâcle, he quit his job and returned to Wisconsin much wiser about the imperatives of American life.

The season was reduced from sixteen to nine games, and the play-off system that produced the Super Bowl contenders was roundly criticized as too generous. Sixteen clubs were given instant-death play-off opportunities at season's end, and the suspicion was that the lack of real "pruning" would affect the quality of the Super Bowl.

There was also the drugs issue. Drug-taking on a daily basis is so commonplace in North America it would have been unreasonable to imagine that there was not a considerable incidence of it in football, where players operated under pressure and were well paid, despite the legitimate claim that they were under-rewarded when compared with baseball and basketball players.

However, the picture of football players smoking marijuana, sniffing cocaine and worse was too shocking for officials at NFL headquarters in New York to even consider. Relentlessly, evidence of drug usage was swept under the carpet. Inevitably, the facts came to the surface. One player, a lineman for the Miami Dolphins and the New Orleans Saints, was arrested for drug dealing. He took his story to *Sports Illustrated*. For those who believed that football was a last redoubt for the finest qualities of American life, the story was one of horror. *Sports Illustrated*'s story described dressing-rooms where drug-taking was a common ritual before games. The League was appalled and talked loosely about tightening procedures, of having "chemical" testing of players. The public, that is, the hard core of football supporters whose habits tend to be no more adventurous than a glass of beer and a shot of rye, were appalled.

FOR A POOR MEXICAN KID, A PEARL

There was also the Al Davis affair. Davis, owner of the Oakland Raiders, decided that he wanted to take his team into the rich greater Los Angeles market. He claimed that a contributory factor to his decision was a series of arguments with the owners of the Oakland Coliseum. Davis claimed the Coliseum had reneged on promises to improve the stadium. He said that he had produced a winning team, one that beat the Philadelphia Eagles in the 1981 Super Bowl, but that the city of Oakland had not responded. Raiders fans were incensed. With some justice, they claimed to be among the most loyal in the land. Pete Rozelle, commissioner of the NFL and a bitter enemy of Davis, fought hard to keep the Raiders out of Los Angeles. Rozelle argued that Davis could not thumb his nose at the League and the fans of Oakland. Davis suggested that Rozelle had other motives, including a personal eye on a new franchise in the vast urban sprawl of southern California. The debate reached the courtroom, and Davis won the early battle, installing his team in the Los Angeles Coliseum, the Los Angeles Rams having moved up the road to Anaheim and Disneyland, appropriately enough, some said. There was the prospect of interminable litigation . . . and a growing sense that football may have waxed too strong, may have assumed too much about its own popularity. A few years earlier a crankish organization known as the Church of Monday Night Football—a celebration of weekly live telecasts of a big Monday night game—seemed to capture the nation's feeling for the game. There was about it a touch of religious fervor. However, cynics (if not heretics) were becoming more voluble as John Riggins arrived at Long Beach airport on a muggy night and promised, "Give me the ball and I'll do the rest."

Riggins certainly did the job. Just as he demolished the Dolphins with his fiercely urgent stride, he also spreadeagled the game's critics. Football may have developed a wart or two, cooked a little "free-base" stimulation in the dressing-room, sniffed an ounce or two of cocaine, showed a flash or two of naked greed, but there was no question that Riggins had performed a remarkable restoration.

A few months later I was in San Francisco and visited Joe Kapp, current coach of the University of California, in his office in Memorial Stadium, high on a hill in Berkeley. In his time Kapp was one of the most colorful and rebellious of National Football League players. He led the University of California to a Rose Bowl championship game and took Minnesota Vikings to a Super Bowl. But Kapp spent the final years of his career in bitter legal dispute with the NFL. He argued that the League operated a closed shop, and though he won his anti-trust action, a jury refused to award him damages, believing that his career was effectively over when he brought an action claiming that club owners had conspired to bar him from the game. I expected to find some lingering bitterness in Kapp, a hint of cynicism. But there was no trace.

"Look what football has done for me," said Kapp as he took my arm and led me to the balcony of his office, which overlooked redwood and eucalyptus trees, and pointed out Golden Gate Bridge shimmering in a heat haze across the bay. "I'm just a poor Mexican kid from Salinas. Football gave me a scholarship to this great university. It changed my life. They say football is America's greatest game, but it's not. The greatest game in America is called opportunity. Football is merely a great expression of it. You bet your ass I believe in what I'm doing here. I won a place in the Rose Bowl, I won the Grey Cup in Canada and I played in the NFL, but the greatest thing that happened to me was getting a degree at this university. Football is fun, and it is something more. It never ceases to amaze me that people can achieve so much once they get a chance, once they get a feel for something."

That day in Berkeley Joe Kapp's main task was persuading eight young football players, mostly from poor black homes, to take a summer course of preparation for their first term as Berkeley freshmen. They all had football scholarships, but, unlike most American universities, Berkeley demands that student athletes maintain acceptable academic standards. Kapp was concerned that some of his best players might fumble the ball in the classroom. He likened the work of educating young athletes to "getting the pearl out of the oyster of football."

It is nearly twenty years since Berkeley was the hotbed of student resistance to conservative thinking in the United States, since the campus echoed with rebellious chants and the nights were illuminated by searchlights and pierced by cries of pain and angry shouts when the police moved in with their nightsticks. The rebels do not parade as much now; the flowers have gone from their hair. Football helmets are fashionable again. Indeed, the university's thrilling victory over its great rival, Stanford, in the fall of 1982 was still a potent memory when I spoke with Kapp six months later. The winning touchdown was the result of extraordinary optimism. In the dying seconds of the game Cal-Berkeley—the Golden Bears—threw seven "lateral" passes, and the player who carried the ball into the end zone ploughed through the Stanford band, which had anticipated the end of play. Stanford's trombone player was a casualty. The significance of Berkeley's triumph was that it was created by the use of the rugby-style lateral pass, long considered a reckless play by orthodox coaches. It is said that it could have happened only under coach Joe Kapp, the brawler from Salinas who used to train for games on tequila and good times.

Kapp said, "People say that touchdown was a miracle. As far as I'm concerned, only God knows about miracles. I only know about telling guys that anything is possible if you go for it. Football's a great vehicle for that message."

Football *is* America. What more could you want from a game? Marshal Foch, at least, would be hard put for an answer.

2

First Battalions

Lawson Fiscus was a proud figure of a man in his Princeton
uniform of one-piece smock, tiger-striped jersey and knee-
length stockings. He exuded physical authority and he
had the running action of a thoroughbred. He was a halfback for
one of the great Ivy League institutions, an aristocrat of the
game. Fiscus knew that he was a great football player, that the
men in the steel mills and collieries of Pennsylvania would pay
scarce dollars to see him stride down the field, ball tucked under
his arm, stunned opponents spinning out of his path.

Fiscus was also a practical man. It may have been true that
college football players tended to look down on the blue-scarred
miners and steel workers, that as late as 1920 college-educated
sports writers publicly sneered as supporters of a professional
team aped the rousing varsity songs in an indoor game at
Madison Square Garden in New York, but Fiscus, as early as
1893, saw that football could get a grip on the working people.
Fiscus was a visionary, and he also needed to eke out his salary
as a school principal. He agreed to become one of the game's first
professionals. He was paid $20 to perform for Greensburg, a
gritty town in the Pennsylvanian steel and coal belt. For many of
his friends this represented an appalling loss of status; it was to
put down an Olympian crown and take on the apron of a
tradesman. But Fiscus did it without complaint and played that
early, savage game with a relish reminiscent of the old bare-
knuckle fighters who delighted the toffs with their marathon
brawls. Fiscus earned every cent of his $20, particularly in the
raw battles with Greensburg's bitter rivals from Latrobe.

Latrobe, a college and residential township in the industrial
sprawl of Pittsburgh, later shifted some of its interest to golf in
recognition of its most famous son, Arnold Palmer, but at the
turn of the century football more perfectly met its emotional
needs. Fiscus was a feared and respected adversary.

For many years the impact of football remained most dramatic on the college fields, first those of the Ivy League places,
Princeton, Yale, Harvard and Rutgers, but spreading quickly to

the American heartland, to Ohio State University, whose stadium in Columbus had by the 1930s become a citadel of the game, to Chicago and to South Bend, Indiana, home of Notre Dame. But it was men such as Fiscus and a fleet, bone-crunching Indian named Isaac Seneca who gave the first clear indication that football would one day become the game of the people, carrying its influence even beyond that of the baseball diamond.

What the professional game needed was a pivotal figure, a man whose celebrity transcended the limits of his own game.

In the 1920s there were five great American sportsmen. The different degrees of their fame tell us much about the sporting history of the nation. In the first rank were Babe Ruth, baseball's peerless slugger; Jack Dempsey, beloved heavyweight champion; the superb golfer Bobby Jones; and the master of the tennis court, Bill Tilden. And then there was Harold "Red" Grange.

Red Grange was a running back for the University of Illinois. He gave football its first overwhelming evidence that it could indeed one day become America's game. He wore the number 77, and his style and pace were so dazzling that soon professional golfers would be calling a round of 77 a Red Grange. He shattered the record statistics in his college career. There was an extraordinary performance on a raw fall day on Franklin Field in Philadelphia. Grange ran with the ball thirty-six times against the University of Pennsylvania; he scored three touchdowns; he won a total of 363 yards. He performed at this freakish level with astonishing consistency. Against the University of Michigan he scored four touchdowns in the first quarter, one of them a 95-yard kick-off return from the shadow of his own posts. He was creating a market that thirty years earlier Lawson Fiscus had seen clearly but knew would take many years to exploit truly. Fiscus's frustration may explain why one day he kicked a fallen opponent square on the jaw.

Inevitably, Grange was a target for the recently revived NFL. He was pursued by a somewhat notorious sportsman and entrepreneur from Chicago named C. C. "Cash-and-Carry" Pyle. Pyle, after much controversy, delivered Grange to the Chicago Bears. In a sense, the spectacle that is now relayed to television screens in millions of homes was given shape and momentum by the running of Grange and the business acumen of Cash-and-Carry Pyle. It was agreed that Grange would be paid $3,000 a game.

Grange shared the Chicago backfield with another legendary figure, Bronko Nagurski. Grange and Nagurski brought a special stride to the Roaring Twenties. Recently Grange, aged 80, told Dave Anderson of the *New York Times*: "It was hard to know what you did when you were running with the football. If you stop and think about it, you get tackled. No running back really knows what he does, he just does it. And whatever he does, it is always different than what the other runners do. If you ask me what I did, I don't have any idea. I had speed, but beyond that I just ran. Those were great years. Some of the finest writers and editors were building up sports right after World War I, when people wanted to relax a little bit, when the country was ready to expand. Maybe it was all built up out of proportion but I'm glad to have been part of it."

The famous sports writer Grantland Rice christened Grange the "Galloping Ghost," and there is no doubt that the extraordinary talent of this dignified young man gave professional football its first claim to respectability. Before Grange's amazing introduction to professional ranks—the Bears had him play eight exhibition games in twelve days—college men shook their heads at activity they judged to be both corrupt and circus-like.

But if pro football was something to disparage over dry martinis, there was no question that within it was something that could attract the man in the street perhaps more profoundly than any other sport. Certainly, the reaction to Chicago's coup was stunning. Thirty-five thousand fans, a record gate for a pro game, braved the wind off Lake Michigan and lined up for Grange's debut for the Bears against the Chicago Cardinals at Wrigley Field, home of the Chicago Cubs baseball team. Two days later 28,000 fans appeared for a game against the Columbus, Ohio Tigers. Cash-and-Carry Pyle rubbed his hands. There was an exhibition game in St Louis against a combination known as Donelly's All Stars. It was pointed out, sourly, that Donelly was an undertaker and that some of his more promising clients had been called to the action. But the turn-outs remained large in Philadelphia, Boston, Washington, and a crowd of more than 70,000 went to the Polo Grounds in New York to see how Grange would deal with the New York Giants. He did not do well, perhaps not surprisingly, considering the pressure of travel and publicity. He had already signed for a Hollywood movie, entitled *Minute to Play*. His fee, $300,000, was astonishing for the times, and his performance revealed a lack of aptitude that was just about total. However, this did not prevent Manhattan's 42nd street from overflowing for the movie's premiere.

Underscoring the whole Grange affair was a quite extraordinary hypocrisy, something that was still visible nearly sixty years later, when a young black from Georgia, Herschel Walker, accepted a contract worth millions of dollars to sign for the New Jersey Generals of the new United States Football League (USFL).

Walker is also a running back, one so gifted that he was thought to have a real chance of a sprinting medal in the 1984 Olympics. But a year before his graduation from the University of Georgia he agreed to join the fledgling USFL. For days he was hounded by the press. His coach at Georgia suggested that by taking the money from the USFL Walker was somehow doing a deal with the devil. Walker, under considerable pressure, at one stage denied that he had signed a contract with the New Jersey Generals. This was soon enough revealed to be wide of the truth, but what was surprising was that long after Red Grange had said yes to the professionals so much was being made of the fact that Walker, whose family were poor sharecroppers in south Georgia, proposed to cash in his athletic ability a year early.

BENEATH THE SURFACE, A SIMMERING RAGE

Amazingly, most of the American press suggested that Walker had fallen from the straight path. My own reaction was outrage. In the mid-1970s I traveled to the Panhandle of Florida to meet Houston McTear, a young black sprinter who was considered a favorite for the 1976 Olympics in Montreal and was also being courted by a division of college football scouts. It was distressing enough to see McTear's living conditions. His family lived in a forlorn cabin beside a swamp. To get there you turned down a rough road, beyond a sawmill and some rusting railtracks. The poignancy lay in the fact that McTear was seen as a commodity as long as he remained one of the world's fastest human beings. If he should fall from that level of fitness, if he should injure himself seriously, he would encounter no moral dilemmas. He would face the rest of his life beside the swamp and the old railtracks. In fact, McTear did injure himself badly on the approach to Montreal. He remains a formidable athlete, but back in the 1970s he had a long and painful recovery. During those years his pot of gold disappeared.

It was, at a very late hour, perhaps another example of the extraordinary value placed on the game of football. There is a stubborn refusal to see the game in the same light as other sports, especially at the college level, where football has been organized with a professionalism as fierce as that in any other corner of American business. There is the story of a brilliant scientist at Ohio State University complaining to the dean that his salary was just a fraction of that of Woody Hayes, the successful but controversial football coach. It is said that the dean pointed to the huge concrete stadium and said to the professor, "When you can fill that place with paying customers, come to me and we'll talk about paying you as much as Woody Hayes." Hayes was eventually fired when, in a moment of frustration, he stepped from the sideline and punched a player.

Walker, producing some dignity under fire, said that in the end he could not turn down the offer. It would change his life and that of his family. His family, after a lifetime of struggle, would be secure. He would set up home with his girlfriend in New York. He would continue to write poetry, and one day he might join the Federal Bureau of Investigation.

Back in the 1920s Red Grange's father, a deputy sheriff in Wheaton, Illinois, advised his son against any exploitation of his athletic gifts. Grange, who was 22, said, "I'm worried and I'm all mixed up." Earlier he had hinted at his awareness that the glory of playing for the University of Illinois might fade quickly enough. As an undergraduate he had subsidized his education by working an ice wagon in his home town. He said that the university would forget him when he didn't have a dollar.

But before any of this, before Fiscus and Grange and Walker, there had to be William Webb Ellis, picking up the ball and running on a misty English field at Rugby school in 1823.

Ellis fathered rugby that historic day. He also set in play enthusiasms that one day would be converted into American football. The first seed was sown by Canadians in 1874. They were from McGill University in Montreal, and they answered a call for football competition from Harvard, the great Boston university having fallen out with Ivy League rivals Yale,

Princeton and Rutgers over "interpretations" of the game. A major problem existed between Harvard and McGill, however. While Harvard did permit a player to pick up the ball and run on occasion, this was by no means the dominating tactic. The "Boston Game," as it was referred to by Yale men, had much more to do with association football or soccer. McGill were enthusiastic rugby players. They tackled and threw the ball, and there was not nearly so much emphasis on kicking.

The universities reached agreement. The first game would be played according to Harvard's rules, the second according to McGill's. After the second game everyone agreed that McGill had the better rules. By comparison with the full-blooded Canadian approach, Harvard's game, which had previously been thought of as splendidly robust, suddenly seemed a touch effete. The truth is that the evolution of American football, more than that of most games, was a matter of chance. Harvard won the first game by three goals to nil and the second was scoreless. It had earlier been agreed that the teams would comprise fifteen players on each side, but some late withdrawals by McGill men brought the number down to eleven. It was found to be a good, practical number.

The American Encyclopedia of Sports deals with the whole affair quite airily, suggesting that what really happened was that American genius had happened on some crude pastime which, while engaging enough on its own level, demanded some serious revision. Says the *Encyclopedia*: "The results were unimportant. The significant thing was that Harvard liked rugby so much that it adopted the rugby rules. Yale and Princeton in turn followed Harvard's action. So the battle was won that was to decide the pattern of a new game . . . a game stemming from rugby but gradually, step by step, departing from rugby in the evolution reflecting American inventive genius and characteristics."

Harvard, having found a game that properly reflected its manliness and aggressive spirit, obviously had to mend relations with suitable opponents, especially its archrivals, Yale. More than a year after the historic meeting between Harvard and McGill, representatives of Yale and Harvard held a conference at Springfield, Massachusetts. The decision was taken to adopt a rugby style of football. Their first game was played under "concessionary rules," and Harvard won quite handsomely. The

Yale men were converted, and quickly enough the definitive American game began to emerge.

Indeed, within ten years the scrum-half, the small, tough man who carried the ball from the rugby "scrum," had been replaced by a figure of more authority, the quarterback. The number of players had been stabilized at eleven, and the scrum had been replaced by the line of scrimmage—which is to say, the "pack" or linemen would stand up and brawl openly rather than link arms and do it surreptitiously and with some sadistic relish. By 1882 "downs" were established. This meant simply that a team had a certain number of opportunities to advance the ball 10 yards, and if they failed, the ball would be handed over to the opposition. The *Encyclopedia of Sports* observes: "These [innovations] were the forerunners of the far-reaching changes having to do with blocking, tackling, forward passing, shifts and formations that were to bring forth a game of such speed, skill, and clever strategic maneuvers to establish football as by far the king of intercollegiate sports throughout the land and bring millions of spectators into the stadiums annually."

What the *Encyclopedia* scarcely dwells on is that the game was being quickly shaped along those lines which so delighted Marshal Foch. There had been hints of military application even when the game languished under the gentler rules of soccer. In a game between Princeton and Rutgers in 1869 a rebel yell was produced by the Princeton players. It was a cry that was said to have terrorized Union soldiers early in the Civil War, and it may be that it also disconcerted Rutgers. Certainly, they lost the game by eight goals. A rough form of soccer was played during the war. There is a woodcut depicting a game at Camp Johnson, Virginia, involving what appears to be the entire First Maryland regiment.

The colleges, inevitably, shaped the game's rules, influenced the patterns of play, perhaps most dramatically in 1913, when the Army team invited a then obscure college from Indiana, Notre Dame, for a game at West Point. Notre Dame, who under the famous coach Knute Rockne would become one of the great symbols of American endeavor, were seen as cannon fodder for the Army in 1913. Physically, the Army had overpowering advantages. But Rockne, who was then a player for the university, a receiver, and Notre Dame's quarterback Gus Dorais had worked together at a holiday camp on the shores of Lake Erie that summer before the Army game. It had given them much

time to practice their execution of the forward pass, a weapon
much neglected at the time.

The Army were cut to pieces by Notre Dame's forward pass.
They might have been savages confronting for the first time a
Gatling gun. The game was never the same again. There would
be reversions to the trenches, there would be the explosive
impact of a running back like Red Grange, but never again
would the potential of the pass be ignored. It might be used
sparingly—as, indeed, it is in modern college football—but it
would always be the glory of the game, its most spectacular
offering to the huge crowds who were beginning to fill new
stadiums like the Yale Bowl, which was opened in 1914.

DREAMS OF NEW CONFLICT . . . AND MAYBE A NICE PROFIT

But if the game was shaped tactically and strategically in the
colleges, if great coaches like Walter Camp and John Heisman
and Amos Alonzo Stagg became giants of the campus, there is no
doubt that it made its deepest thrust into the imagination of
America on professional fields. Lawson Fiscus, a mature warrior, most clearly pointed to a future when the NFL would sign a
contract worth $5 billion with television networks, when a
football league, the USFL, would be created solely for the vast
appetite of football's television market.

This kind of commercial potential was first realized by Red
Grange and Cash-and-Carry Pyle, but more than twenty years
earlier men like Connie Mack, whose Philadelphia Athletics
were a cornerstone of the first attempt to launch a National
Football League, had been dreaming similar dreams. Mack's
coach was Blondy Wallace, a character who would not have met
the stringent ethical requirements demanded by the modern
league. Wallace found his life's work in breezy Atlantic City,
where he revelled in the title "King of the Bootleggers." The
Athletics made a niche for themselves in history playing a
floodlit game in Elmira, in upstate New York. And then there
was Leo Lyons, whose passion for the game took the Rochester
Jeffersons into the NFL. The Jeffersons, named for a street in the
New York state city, were Lyons's lifework. It was said that he
could have had a successful career in politics or commerce, but
his vocation was to make his team the most powerful force in

professional sport. He had his moments, coming close to signing the phenomenal Grange and once, in an emergency, signing a physically impressive Chicago mounted policeman shortly before a game.

Lyons was maybe the definitive football man of those pioneering days. He was part-dreamer, part-huckster. He spent the prime of his life scuffling to pay his bills and keep the Rochester Jeffersons out of bankruptcy. Half his time was spent soothing bank managers, half seeking out talent to make good promises of spectacular entertainment. He patched up teams and persuaded the public that it was seeing athletic perfection. He was driven to distraction by the loose sense of professionalism displayed by many of his players. He faced down strike meetings called in hotel lobbies in half a dozen cities. He poured black coffee down the throats of feckless, hung-over "stars," cajoled broken veterans on to the field for one last run at glory and, long after it was prudent, he would himself dress for action, a child-man forever locked into the dreams of his youth.

There is a photograph of Lyons taken in 1914. He stands proudly in front of a ramshackle grandstand. The nickname of his club, the Jeffs, is emblazoned across the front of his jersey, as it might have been his heart, and on his face is the true contentment of a warrior about to go into battle. There is no hint here that at the back of his mind is the worry that next week he will be unable to pay the wages of his warriors, perhaps not even those of the women who wash the uniforms and that the whole elaborate enterprise is built on not much more than his own extraordinary optimism.

Lyons's consolations came later, much later, and were not without poignancy and some bitterness. Some sixty years after he stood on the frozen field in Rochester and smiled at the camera, Lyons worked as a part-time and somewhat erratic historian for the NFL, the most profitable organization in the entire history of professional sport. He documented the fabulous wealth of the League, a wealth he had anticipated as clearly as Henry Ford had foreseen the impact of the Model T. But, unlike Ford, Lyons was born at least several decades before his time. In his old age he saw rich men, men of inherited wealth or money conjured from industry and commerce, buy football clubs, acquisitions that were sops to vanity or solid investments. And it was then that he felt some bitterness. He thought of his own adventurous days when a journey to a steel mill or colliery in Pennsylvania to recruit some budding talent was undertaken for the good of his team and not merely for the turning of a dollar. Robert Smith, in his *Illustrated History of Pro Football*, tells of the time when Lyons hoped to rescue himself from the jaws of bankruptcy with a game in Orange, New Jersey. He had been given a guarantee of $1,200, which would have granted him a small amount of liquidity at season's end. His players had agreed to take wage cuts. But the life-saving game was a disaster. Frank Matteo, Lyons's celebrated tackle, had his elbow shattered. A guard, Charlie Strack, broke his collarbone. Worst of all, Lyons lost his crowd-pleasing receiver Gene Bedford with a crushed femur. Strack and Matteo were serious losses but they were linemen, concerned more with production than with work at center-stage. Bedford was a prime asset, a man who delighted the fans with his electric running and safe hands. Lyons was, briefly, a broken man as he escorted Bedford home to Rochester, easing his stretcher into a Pullman. Bedford never thrilled another crowd. He remained in the hospital for six months, and the bills were sent to Lyons, whose check from the game promoter in New Jersey promptly bounced. But then there would be a new season and new prospects soon enough.

Joe Horrigan, curator of the NFL's Hall of Fame, recalls: "Leo had very big dreams, and in his old age it was a though he could never detach himself from those days with the Rochester Jeffs. Once his team lost its place in the NFL [in 1925] he seemed to turn away from reality. He had come very close to making it. Perhaps if he had signed Red Grange, everything would have turned out differently for him, but I guess sport is full of maybes. One thing you have to concede to Leo Lyons. He knew that one day football would be *the* game. I suppose his main problem was that he was always under-financed."

At a distance, and through the evidence of dusty pages and old prints, there is no doubt that Leo Lyons cuts a brave, perhaps even a noble figure. His idea was to capture the public, grow rich from its enthusiasm, but then he did believe passionately in his product. He was no snake-oil salesman. He also had his place in history when he attended the founding of the first national league in 1920. Curiously, he always insisted that the meeting, held in a car salesroom in Canton, Ohio, was held in 1919. Says Horrigan, "Leo had the date wrong and maybe his own significance at the meeting. But he was there. He did make a contribution."

His contribution was perhaps that of a dreamer, but without such dogged dreamers the incredible wealth of modern professional football would never have accrued. In fact, while Lyons was fighting for survival in upstate New York, the professional game was to make its most significant early thrust a little further west, in Ohio, specifically in Canton and Massillon. These small cities, separated by just 8 miles of rolling farmland, had developed a mutual hostility as sharp as anything that had existed earlier between Greensburg and Latrobe in Pennsylvania. The hostility flowed from action on the football field. It was a rivalry that gathered greater momentum than anything that had gone before. It sucked in more resources and would ultimately provide the hard evidence that professional football had the potential to set up a National League embracing the great cities from coast to coast.

WILLIE HESTON'S ORDEAL: A BAD DAY IN CHICAGO

Massillon, who played their games on the grounds of a mental asylum—altogether appropriately, Cantonites insisted—made the first moves toward overt professionalism. They made no secret of the fact that they fielded four mercenaries from Pennsylvania in their Ohio State championship game with Akron in 1903. Canton's response was never less than competitive, and this was spectacularly so in 1906. The "Tigers" brought down Willie Heston, a superb running back of the University of Michigan, whose team had dominated college football at the turn of the century. Heston, who graduated in 1904, had been inactive for two years, and when he arrived in Ohio it was fairly clear that the Corinthian figure who had so dazzled the varsity fields had lost some of its splendor.

It was reported that Heston was seen leaving a bar at 2 a.m. on the day of the game. It was also noted that he appeared to be a good 20 pounds overweight. Heston waved away the doubters. He was Willie Heston of Michigan, and God help anyone who stepped in his path. He would be worth every cent of his $600 match fee. The game was still young when the Massillon crowd decided that Heston had left the best of his stuff in Michigan.

Massillon's own mercenaries, some of whom had good college reputations, launched themselves at Heston whenever he touched the ball, which initially was from every line of scrimmage when Canton had the ball. Heston did not gain a yard that frosty afternoon. Robert Smith reports that he played with courage in a defensive role, but the truth was that in those days not even a Willie Heston could provide $600 worth of defense in just one game. Massillon triumphed by 14 points to 4. Heston slipped out of town, his bones aching and his brain recoiling from the fact that the cronies who had slapped his back just a few hours before had disappeared. He had never had much appetite for the professional game, and he would live to regret the fact that he ever tried to reproduce the glory of his college days. He played once more, in Chicago, his status and his fee reduced by events in Ohio. There was no resurrection for Willie Heston. In Chicago he broke his leg.

Historically, there was a small place for Heston in the professional game. There was no doubt that his journey to Ohio had galvanized the rivalry, brought new levels of competition. Edward Stewart, editor of the Massillon newspaper, which ran daily editorials questioning the good name of Canton manhood, organized the town's team with a fury, inspiring his Canton friend and rival Bill Day to equally frantic and expensive team-building. There were some ludicrous aspects to the rivalry. In those days it was normal for the eleven players to operate "both ways," or take on both offensive and defensive duties. Today a team has quite separate offensive and defensive units, plus "special teams" for kicking, punting and returning the ball from opposing kicks. So it was bizarre, back in 1905, to see as many as forty players assembled along the touchline by Massillon and Canton. "The idea," reports Joe Horrigan, "was to sign up players even if you didn't plan to play them in the game. You would at least deny the opposition the chance of signing up a good player. It does seem incredible now, but those guys took the game pretty seriously."

Inevitably, the drain on personal resources was too great, and Stewart and Day were probably relieved when the game was obliged to make a strategic withdrawal. The Canton Bulldogs were briefly disbanded. The crisis came when the *Massillon Independent* reported that two of the town's victories over Canton were tainted. The *Independent* claimed that Canton's coach

Blondy Wallace, who had moved from Pennsylvania to Ohio on his raffish, roundabout route to retirement in Atlantic City, had organized a betting coup. Canton had thrown the game, said the newspaper. Wallace wrote an indignant letter, pleaded his innocence, but it was noted that he first left town and that the envelope that carried his letter bore the postmark of an extremely obscure place.

Around Canton and Massillon pro football had become overheated. The supporters of the teams had turned the short rail journey between the cities into something from the Crusades. Fist fights spilled into the streets. The betting scandal is a specter that still haunts professional football, Art Schlichter, a young quarterback of Ohio State University and Baltimore Colts, being suspended by the NFL in 1983, after it was revealed that he had run up nearly $1 million worth of gambling debts. Back in 1906 the men who had to pick up the bills decided that the best thing would be to suspend the game for a while, let passions cool and checking accounts recover.

Certainly, the Canton Bulldogs benefited from the respite. Quickly enough, feelings of disgust and betrayal paled beside vivid memories of wild betting, even wilder drinking and, as it happened, some superb collisions on the field. Elsewhere in Ohio the growth of the professional game had been steady, and when the first National League was formed five of the eleven founding clubs were from the state—Canton, Akron Steels, Cleveland Panthers, Columbus Panhandles and the Dayton Triangles. Of these clubs Columbus had a distinct advantage in the matter of team work. Six of the Columbus players were supplied by the Nessers, an immigrant family from Alsace. Ted Nesser Junior played with his strapping son Fred. They were an extraordinary bunch, the Nessers. Off the field they worked hard on the railway lines; on it they marshalled vast peasant strength and ran fearlessly into the heart of the enemy lines. But in 1915 the Nessers were eclipsed, as were all professional football players across the land, by the most important signing in the history of the Canton club, perhaps in all of football.

In 1915 Canton signed Jim Thorpe. They also signed Pete Calac, a slim, handsome flier who, like Thorpe, had played for the Carlisle Indian Institute in Pennsylvania, which boasted of the finest pure talent in college football. Calac was an impressive performer, but his misfortune was to arrive at the same time as

Thorpe, who, if you listen to the old men, was maybe the greatest football player of all time.

In 1950 Jim Thorpe was voted the best player of the half-century. There is no more poignant story in sport. When Canton signed him he was a national celebrity several times over. In 1912 the big Indian carried the pentathlon and decathlon gold medals at the Stockholm Olympics. When King Gustav V handed Thorpe his medals he said, "You are the greatest athlete in the world." Thorpe smiled shyly and said, "Thanks, King." Thorpe's pride remained uncomplicated for just seven months. It took that long for an Olympic committee to investigate an informant's charge that Thorpe was not entitled to his medals. He had received $2 a game for playing minor league baseball in 1909 and 1910. Thorpe was bemused. He could not relate the pittance he had received to his efforts in Stockholm. The baseball belonged to another time in his life, another season. For Stockholm he had shaped a new and rigorous life, submitted himself to sacrifices, some of them not easy for a young man who had already tasted some of the pleasures of life, not least the exhilarating effects of alcohol. Thorpe, who also liked to gamble, might have left the matter to the strange values of the Olympic committee, a little foggily perhaps, and proceeded with his football career. But his family and some of his Sac and Fox tribespeople felt the injustice strongly, and they worried it down the years, even as Thorpe drifted into bouts of alcoholism. His daughter Gail fought most ferociously for a return of the medals, and it was to her that Juan Antonio Samaranch re-presented the medals in 1982. Thorpe had died in his trailer in Lomita, California, twenty-nine years earlier.

Thorpe played football into his forties, but by then he had become a parody of his old self. An Associated Press reporter provided a bleak account of his last game, in Chicago: "The Chicago Bears routed their ancient rivals, the Chicago Cardinals, 34–0 in the annual Thanksgiving Day game at Wrigley Field today. Jim Thorpe played a few minutes for the Cardinals but was unable to get anywhere. In his forties and musclebound, Thorpe was a mere shadow of himself."

"BORN TO PLAY, TO RUN AND TO TACKLE"

. The last years of his life were nightmarish but perhaps only for those who had revered him as a superlative athlete. Thorpe himself seemed not to experience too much pain. Certainly, there are many pictures of a round-faced Indian smiling benignly at the camera. A former teammate was asked about the kind of drink that Thorpe preferred. "Anything he could get his hands on," was the reply. For a while he shuffled around Hollywood, getting occasional work as an extra in westerns and the odd hour or two as an adviser on "football scenes." He was variously reported to be digging ditches, trying to trade on his old celebrity, being fined for drunken driving. "The truth is," said a companion of his youth, "Jim lived to play and run, to kick and tackle. When he could no longer do that any more, I guess a lot of the meaning went out of life for him." He was divorced twice, ran up gambling debts, moved around. It was a classic example of a great athlete disintegrating when he could no longer hear the roar of the crowd. But few men had heard the cheers for so long.

Thorpe was prodigious at every aspect of the game. He could punt the ball from one end of the field to the other, and often a side attraction to an exhibition game would be a half-time kicking duel between Thorpe and the best the opposition could provide. Thorpe invariably won. He was utterly ruthless in the matter of providing himself with an edge, some opponents even alleging that he inserted pieces of steel into the padding around his vast shoulders. It was nothing to see Thorpe run through a team, a grin spreading across his broad face. Jimmy Conzelman, a contemporary of Thorpe who had faced such rushes, declared as late as 1963, "Jim Thorpe could have made any team in the NFL today. What's more, he would have been the best player on that team. I might also add that he would have been the best player in the entire League." George Sullivan's *A to Z of Pro Football* quotes from a *New York Times* report of a Thorpe performance for the Carlisle Institute against the Army: "Thorpe is the athletic marvel of the age. At times the game itself was almost forgotten while the spectators gazed on Thorpe, the individual, to wonder at his prowess. He simply ran wild as the cadets tried in vain to stop his progress. It was like trying to stop a shadow."

It was thus considerably more than a football player that Canton acquired when the club's new owner, Jim Cusack, agreed to pay Thorpe $250 a game. Thorpe strode around Canton as a king or perhaps a war chief. He was amiable enough off the field, but on it he never disguised his love of winning or his enjoyment of his own physical power. One of his sharpest pleasures was to hit a receiver at full pace as he moved to catch the ball. Thorpe would hit with crunching power at the last possible moment and invariably the receiver would be flattened. As the victim lay groaning, Thorpe, a natural if rather heavy comedian, would lean over him and declare, "A man could get hurt playing this game. If he don't take care." Cusack was delighted with his investment. He said, "Some of my business advisers frankly predicted that I was leading the Bulldogs into bankruptcy by paying Jim the enormous sum of $250 a game. But the deal paid off beyond my greatest expectations. Jim was an attraction as well as a player. All the fans wanted to see the big Indian in action."

When the National League was formed in 1920 it seemed to everyone that Thorpe was the natural choice for president. Pro football might still be disreputable; it might reek with suspicions of betting fixes; it might be haphazardly organized by often shady characters: but if it could offer a Thorpe as president, it was not without merit. The Ohio clubs were joined by Buffalo Americans, Chicago Tigers, Rochester Jeffs, Decatur Staleys, Hammond Pros and the Rock Island Independents. Thorpe was the colorful figurehead in Canton. The brains and the drive were provided largely by another, younger man, a man for whom the fantasies of Leo Lyons would become a reality for more than sixty years. The young man was George Halas, founder of the Chicago Bears, who would eventually be known throughout football simply as Papa Bear. At the meeting in Canton, Halas was manager, coach and player of the Decatur Staleys, a team sponsored by a starch company. Halas was just 25 years old when he want to Canton, but already he had clear ideas about the league of the future.

It would be a league rising above its tribal origins. It would have glamor and prestige and perhaps even respectability, though that was not one of Halas's priorities. Respectability could wait, as it did in all areas of dynamic growth in North America. Halas had all the right qualities for such empire-building. As a coach and administrator he was sharp, unscrupulous and always eager to innovate. As a player he was shrewd and fearless. It was a formidable combination of qualities, and one day it would prompt football historian Arthur Daley to write, "George Halas didn't invent football, it just seemed that way." It was a reasonable impression, such was the weight of Halas's contribution. When the Staley Starch Company withdrew its support of a league that seemed to be in almost instant financial difficulties, Halas moved his team to Chicago. By 1922 the League had swollen to eighteen clubs, and Halas's Chicago Bears finished second. He was a relentless recruiter of talent—preferably cheap talent that had slipped through the coverage of rival scouts—and the passion of his own play was a potent factor in the club's growth. In 1923 Halas grasped an opponent's fumble cleanly and ran 98 yards, a record that stood for forty-nine years.

In 1925 Halas did his vital business with Cash-and-Carry Pyle and dispatched Red Grange across the continent, pushing the great player relentlessly, demanding that he worked for every cent of his signing fee. Quickly Halas and his team became the bedrock of the League. He installed the Bears in Wrigley Field, a well established baseball ground in Chicago's North Side. By the late 1920s Halas was spent as a player, and in 1929 he also resigned as coach, deciding it was time to step back and take a new perspective.

T-TIME: PAPA BEAR SEES THE FUTURE

His withdrawal to the executive office lasted just four years. The lure of the touchline, the mystique of a game in which a coach had the power to decide the action as clearly as a front-line commander, was too strong. Halas returned refreshed, his brain teeming with new tactical approaches. He had always flirted with the "T" formation, which is the basic offensive formula used in the modern game and means simply that the quarterback receives the ball directly from between the legs of the crouching center and has the option of handing off to a running back or stepping back and throwing to a receiver. Before Halas developed the "T" the routine pattern in the professional game was the single-wing, which required the center to toss the ball back 5 yards, an arrangement that made him extremely vulnerable to the rush of opposing linemen and gave the quarterback nothing like the range of alternatives provided by the "T." Halas proved, devastatingly, that the "T" was the future.

The point was made most dramatically in the NFL final against the Washington Redskins in 1940. The Bears, controlled by Sid Luckman, a physically unimpressive quarterback with a wonderful knack of masking his intentions, produced a performance that was described as "awesome." Luckman had a superb throw; he propeled the ball as easily as a champion dart thrower might dispatch his arrow. The Redskins were cut to pieces. Luckman, a New Yorker who was at first resistant to Halas's claim that civilized life existed west of the Hudson River, won the freedom of Chicago with his surgical skills against Washington. The score was 73–0. Had Halas withdrawn from professional football as dusk covered that battlefield, his place in the history of the game would have been secure. As it was, he decided that perhaps his talents could be used in a wider conflict and he promptly joined the US Navy.

Not everybody hailed Halas as the great innovator. Amos Alonzo Stagg claimed his own playbook had been delved into by Halas—and it was a playbook that had been in operation as far back as 1894. Stagg, who was 103 years old when he died in 1965, was coach of the University of Chicago for forty years. He then put in a brief stint of fifteen years with the University of the Pacific. With Walter Camp and John Heisman, Stagg was a key figure in the development of the college game, but he was less than generous in his claim that Halas was doing no more than dusting old tactics. In fact, Stagg may have been driven by old wounds. In 1922 he had argued quite bitterly against professional football, and the *Chicago Herald and Examiner* headlined an interview with the old coach thus: "The [Big Ten College] Conference Will Break the Professional Football Menace." The NFL's official history later pointed out with some relish that this was the first eight-column headline ever granted the professional game by a major city newspaper. The truth was that Halas had reshaped the game. Wonderful tactics can be fashioned on blackboards, but it takes a special force and insight to turn them into the coinage of victory. This Halas did with dynamic force in 1940, and when the challenge of Hitler and the Emperor of

Japan was resolved satisfactorily, Halas returned to Chicago and started all over again.

His first move was to win the 1946 NFL title, his Bears beating the New York Giants by 24 points to 14. The Bears were a force as long as he operated on the touchline, but competition stiffened steadily, and the national titles would become less easily acquired. He won one more, in 1963, and then retired from coaching in 1969. He had done much to translate the romance of the college game into a rigorous code for mature professionals. Part visionary, part martinet, he had introduced the policy of daily practice, not so much because of the opportunities it presented for tuning fitness and game preparation but also because of the military discipline it implied. The rhythm of the game was so fast, so demanding, that the challenge of it had to be re-emphasized on a daily basis. It was unnatural to deliver so much punishment to the human body. Halas concluded that preparation had to be extreme and that it had to be both mental and physical. Without such a regime his players would slide from the necessary levels of discipline. They would be like many professional baseball players, excessive in their lifestyle, naturally rebellious. They would follow the example of the great Babe Ruth, whose superb achievements were balanced precariously on rampaging appetites for food, drink and female companionship.

Halas once observed drily, "A big city is filled with varied attractions for a young athlete. If a player has to report for morning practice, he won't do much playing of a different sort at night." It was a wise observation in the city of countless speakeasies, of Al Capone and the Hotsy Totsy club and an invigorating wind off Lake Michigan.

Halas's obsessions spawned other trends. He was the first to make the analysis of film standard practice before and after games. Today even the high school coach has a film room attached to his office. Once I was permitted to sit in on a session of film analysis in a coach's room. It was rather as though an infidel had been granted entrance to a holy place. The only stipulation was that I should not name names as the professional careers of individual players were being shaped by minute examination of a hundred reruns. Week by week the fate of players is decided at these sessions. A player is cut from the club because some sharp-eyed coach has seen him, or believed he has

seen him, malingering in some frantic jumble of action. The
killing evidence is of "loafing." A player may be forgiven for a
missed assignment, a faulty decision—though not often—but if it
is sensed that his commitment is in doubt, well, the odds are that
there will be an empty place in the dressing-room for a day or
two.

There is an old football joke. A journalist asks, "What did you
think of the game, coach?" and the coach replies, "I won't know
until I've seen the film." Halas's own picture of the game was
uniquely complete. He was born when Lawson Fiscus and
Fiscus's rival for the title of the game's first professional, Pudge
Heffelfinger of Yale, were making the early moves to com-
mercialize the game. And in the summer of 1983 he was still
chief executive of the Chicago Bears. It was not an honorary
title, though some of the club's most passionate fans might have
wished that it were so. There was no doubt that some of the
game had passed him by, but there he was, still riding at the
helm of a powerful club in an age when the League had waxed
stronger than any of those in the car salesroom back in Canton in
1920 could ever have imagined. In 1983 a new football league,
the USFL, had negotiated its first season. The League had been
floated by a three-year contract from ABC television, and
though attendances at the games had been erratic, there was a
clamor for fresh franchises at the end of the season. Still another
league, the International Football League, announced that it too
would clamber on the bandwagon. Some even saw an exhibition
game between St Louis Cardinals and the Minnesota Vikings in
London as the first step towards a truly international league, one
National Football League official speculating headily about
Super Bowls in Tokyo and Berlin and Rome.

None of this obscured some harsher realities. Drug-taking in
the dressing-room had apparently become endemic, and some of
the more reflective football people wondered if the game had not
taken its grip on the American public a little for granted. But for
George Halas the essential fact was that his life's work had
realized all the rewards for which he had hoped sixty-three years
earlier, when he traveled to Ohio. The Bears might no longer be
major challengers for league honors, their appeal resting largely
on the ability of a superb running back named Walter Payton,
but it was still true that season tickets for the games at Soldier
Field were eagerly sought. It was also true that the club received

more than $13 million from television resources before it sold one ticket, one bag of popcorn, one can of beer. Football was an American dream. It was instant money, instant fame.

When George Halas returned to his home on Chicago's Lakeshore Drive after a spell in the hospital early in 1983 a newspaper ran the headline "Papa Bear Cheats Death Again." America's game had flooded the old man with gifts. It had given him celebrity, a rich living for himself and his family. Was it now bestowing one last gift? Had Halas become part of the game, indestructible, immortal? When he died in the fall of the year, there was a sense of shock out of all proportion to the event.

3

Myths of War

There is no doubt that football errs on the side of the portentous and the complex. Fierce young linebackers from sleepy farming hamlets in the Deep South have been transformed into kittens by their first sight of the "playbook." The playbook describes in vast detail, and with diagrams, the moves favored by the team coach. Beside these tomes Montgomery's notes before El Alamein might have been scrawled on a postcard or two. As a training camp proceeds new moves are often stapled into the playbook, and sometimes one already absorbed by the players is rewritten. Glen Jackson, a veteran linebacker in the Canadian Football League, says, "It's pitiful to see some of the kids trying to deal with the playbook. It's as though they have been given some obscure formula in a foreign language. Their eyes glaze over. Their bodies are battered and their brains are numb. Sure, they get overloaded."

It is in the huddle, where the quarterback lowers his head and barks out commands to his clustered troops, that the inflation and the weight of the playbook either lives or crumbles under the pressure of action and, perhaps, the vulnerability of young, overstretched minds.

More often than not, the game's creators of mystique would like you to believe, the playbook crumbles. Ahmad Rashad blew away some of the mythology in a series of articles written with *Sports Illustrated*'s Frank Deford before the 1982 season. A graduate of the University of Oregon, Rashad had always been skeptical of many of football's values, and he caused a considerable stir among officials of the conservative NFL and his own club, Minnesota Vikings, when he decided to adopt his Muslim name. He had been known as "Bobby Moore" in his days as a college star.

In his articles with Deford Rashad questioned every aspect of the game—its discipline, its lingering color bar, its medieval industrial relations, its inability to deal rationally with the drug problem and its sometimes breathtaking pomposity. He also spoke movingly of the game's rewards, the sense of fulfillment he found in making the big catches, in running a pattern that dissected a team so utterly that the touchdown was a formality. He also enjoyed his status as a veteran, a man who could prove to the annual influx of big, quick young men that he was still worth his place at the top of the game.

Rashad was a celebrity, a loose, bright man who formed his own opinions rather than accepting those handed down via the coach's bullhorn. He was withering about the playbook, its vanities and its demands on players.

Declared Rashad, "As soon as the coach says, 'Tell the quarterback to call this play,' the guy carrying the play in [from the sideline to the huddle] starts thinking about what *he* does. Let's say he is supposed to tell the quarterback to call Flanker Right 62X and Flanker Fly, which is a pass. Let's say the guy carrying the play in is a running back. All he starts thinking about is what pattern he runs on that play and in what direction. By the time he gets to the huddle he knows exactly what he's supposed to do on Flanker Right 62X and Flanker Fly, only he doesn't remember what the play is, so he can go and do it.

"Or this happens. A guy runs in with the play. As he runs, he keeps saying the words over and over to himself, the way you do with a new telephone number when you're looking for a pencil. Then, as soon as he gets to the huddle, before he draws another breath, he spits it out, 'FLANKERRIGHTSIXTY-TWOANDFLANKERFLY.' He's so relieved to have done his job, the whole thing goes right out of his mind. Only the quarterback didn't hear clearly. So he says, 'What?'

"Another reason the guy bringing the play in gets it wrong is that he knows that everyone in the huddle wants him to get it wrong. This is because they all always get it wrong when they bring it in. Besides if anyone screws up on a wrong play, then you can blame the poor sucker who brought it in. So you get it wrong to satisfy peer pressure. Isn't it wonderful to be in the NFL, at the height of your profession?

"We've all been trained to be robots in the quarterback huddle, so when he claps his hands and says, 'Break,' we all rush up to the line and do whatever comes to mind on the nonexistent Split Left X and Flanker Stick 52. Luckily, I'm the split left part. I split *far* left."

Rashad, heading for a career in TV journalism, was perhaps showing an early talent for a good angle and dramatic effect, but his *Sports Illustrated* diaries were filled with dry humor, and on his central point about the unnecessary complexity of most "game plans" there could be little effective counter from within the game. There is a high school in Ohio which employs eighteen football coaches. You may think that this is a misprint. It is not. That's right, eighteen coaches. There are coaches for conditioning, offensive and defensive coordinators, corner back coaches, quarterback coaches, linebacker coaches, running back coaches. There are men who work on motivation, on discipline (even, now, on psychology), and it is also true that otherwise excellent young football players are turned away because they fail to meet some arbitrary demand of the stopwatch or the scales.

It may be that the force of modern life, the changes in American society that make the questioning of discipline a virtue rather than a sign of some irredeemable flaw in character, will change the coach–player relationship fundamentally in the next few years. Certainly, there are already signs of this. Hugh Campbell, a quiet, reflective man who learned his football in small colleges in the United States, then moved to Canada for a record-breaking reign as coach of the all-powerful Edmonton Eskimos—under Campbell they won the Grey Cup for five successive years—was appointed coach of the United States Football League franchise in Los Angeles in 1982. His salary was more than $250,000 a year. When he arrived in LA it was as though he had dropped in from outer space.

The *Los Angeles Times* carried a long feature article about this extraordinary football character who had come from the north with strange ideas about how to treat a player. Campbell himself said, "Too often football forgets that it is involved in human beings, people as vulnerable as anyone else walking the street. Coaches forget that the players are like everyone else. They've grown up in an age when you don't take your orders without thinking about them.

"These days you have to relate the game to the rest of life. If a guy drops the ball, you have to accept that he didn't plan to do that, and nothing you say can get back that opportunity. What you have to decide is whether the fellow can play the game. If he can, you look for the positive. You certainly don't treat him as you would a schoolkid."

Dave Cutler, a field goal kicker whose nerve and skill held good for Campbell in many vital situations, summed up for me the coach's quality one evening after practice under a prairie moon. Campbell had already received the call to Los Angeles, and this had been one of his last practice sessions with the Edmonton veterans. Said Cutler, "I just hope that Hughie has success in the States because I believe he represents the future of football. Under his kind of leadership the game can adapt to a new society. I'll always remember one thing he said to me, quite soon after he had taken over. I had a crucial field goal attempt at Taylor Field [the ground of the Saskatchewan Rough Riders in Regina] and there was a very tricky field goal. The game depended on that kick. Well, I misread the wind and the ball went wide. I was inconsolable in the dressing-room. I just sat down in the shower, staring at the floor. Eventually, Hughie poked his head into the shower and said, 'Hey, never be so arrogant as to think a football game was ever won or lost by one man.' I thought it made the point about what we were doing quite brilliantly."

So far Campbell remains something of a visionary.

Most NFL coaches believe that if they let discipline slip, they are lost. It is an argument that even the naturally skeptical Ahmad Rashad might not oppose totally. Certainly, he was shocked to find some teammates preparing drugs in their hotel room a few hours before an important game—so shocked that he immediately called a friend and ex-player in order to express his outrage and to seek advice about how he should react. Rashad has not advanced solutions; he has merely held up a light to some murky and confused areas.

"REALLY, A SIMPLE GAME — A REAL SIMPLE GAME"

All Rashad was really saying was that there is a tendency to inflate the subtleties of American football; that a mystique has grown around even the most basic of maneuvers. Everybody does it. It has become an industry. "Forget that the rulebook runs to some sixty-eight pages," I was once told by a colleague, "and forget that an American writer named Paul Zimmerman elevated it to the lofty heights of nuclear physics or advanced calculus when he wrote a book entitled *The Thinking Man's Guide to Pro Football*. It's really a simple game. Yes, a real simple game."

The intent of the game is easily understood by anyone familiar with soccer, rugby or any of the many court games that are derived from the same basic objective: to score points by moving a ball from one end of the playing area to the other.

The ball in this case is the same shape as a rugby ball, although it has more pointed ends and a smaller circumference, thus making it easier to throw.

The game of football combines elements of soccer and rugby. Points can be scored by running or passing the ball (touchdowns) or by kicking (field goals and extra points). Defense is also rewarded with points in the case of a safety touch, awarded to a team that traps the opposition behind its own goal line.

A football game begins with one team kicking the ball to the other team, which attempts to advance the ball as far upfield as possible before it is tackled by a member (or more likely members) of the kicking team.

The kick-off completed, play begins in earnest. The offensive team must move the ball toward the opposing goal, and it accomplishes this by either running or passing the ball forward. A team is given a series of four plays, or downs, in which to advance the ball 10 yards. Each time the team advances 10 yards, it is awarded a first down and a new series of four downs.

The ball is put into play by the center, who is one of the five interior linemen. The center "snaps" or passes the ball through his legs to the quarterback. Usually, the quarterback stands directly behind the center and the ball is placed directly in the quarterback's hands. On other occasions, the quarterback may line up in a "shotgun" formation, where he will stand 5 yards behind the center, who must then toss the ball backwards through his legs.

Once he receives the ball, the quarterback has a number of options. He can run with the ball and hand off to one of his running backs or he can throw the ball downfield to one of his receivers.

On passing plays the quarterback must remain behind the line of scrimmage when he is throwing the ball, and the ball must be caught in the air by an eligible receiver who is in bounds. If the ball touches the ground first or is caught out of the playing area, it is ruled as incomplete pass and the team loses a down.

The process of moving the ball toward the opposing goal continues until the offensive team scores or until the defense team can force a change in possession.

There are two ways for an offensive team to score points. The first is a touchdown, which is accomplished by running or passing the ball successfully into the end zone. A touchdown is worth 6 points and entitles a team to try for a bonus point after a touchdown. The team scoring a touchdown is given one play from the 5-yard line and must kick the ball through the uprights at the end of the field. The rules also permit a team to run or pass the ball into the end zone for the extra point, but kicking is the normal method for attempting this point because such attempts usually have a high success rate.

When a team moves the ball close to the opposing end zone but cannot advance the ball any further, it may elect to try a field goal, which is worth 3 points. This is a placement kick, in which the holder takes a snap from the center and places the ball upright on the ground about 7 yards behind the line of scrimmage. The place kicker then attempts to kick the ball through the uprights.

Possession can change in a number of ways. If a team fails to advance 10 yards in its four allotted downs, it must surrender possession to the defensive team. The usual method of exchanging possession in this matter is by a kick or "punt" on fourth down. The offensive team will kick the ball away rather than gamble on a fourth-down play. If the offensive team has only a short way to go to complete its 10-yard advance, it may gamble. If it moves the ball successfully, the offensive team retains possession with a new series of downs. If it fails to advance the ball, the defensive team takes possession.

The ball may also change possession on "turnovers." Turnovers are either fumbles, in which the defensive team recovers a ball dropped by an offensive player, or interceptions, in which a defensive player catches a pass intended for an offensive player.

A game consists of four quarters, each consisting of fifteen minutes' playing time. Unlike soccer, the clock is stopped frequently, and games often run as long as three hours. The clock is stopped after first downs, after an incomplete pass, after a runner has gone out of bounds and at various times to fit in radio or television commercials.

The teams change ends after each quarter, and a great deal of strategy is based on a team's decision to defend one end or the other. Wind, sunlight and other factors are taken into consideration when a team chooses which end it wishes to defend.

There is a fifteen-minute intermission at half-time and this time is generally given over to the "half-time show," which features marching bands, baton twirlers and cheerleaders.

One of the first mysteries of the game for a newcomer is the regular interchange of offensive and defensive units. For followers of soccer and rugby the idea that a club may field eleven offensive specialists when it has the ball, then replace them with eleven defenders the moment it loses possession, seems both expensive and redundant. What happened to the concept of the all-round athlete? In the old days football players performed both offensively and defensively, but as resources grew and tactics became more sophisticated at every level, separate units became commonplace and in time the "special team" was considered essential. The special teams, often augmented by members of the other units, are responsible for punt and kick-off and field goal situations. There is an element of desperation about many special team men. The function of the unit is vital and involves high-speed collision as blockers confront marauders eager to prevent the punt or kick receiver from making serious progress downfield.

The strategic priorities of the principal units can be outlined briefly enough.

OFFENSE

Woody Hayes, the excitable, ultimately self-destructive coach at Ohio State University, used to say there were three things that could happen when you threw a football and two of them were bad. That advice notwithstanding, professional football teams are passing more than at any time in the history of the game.

For years the trend in professional football was for teams to run on the first down of any offensive series. Subsequent strategy was based on the result of that play. If a team picked up 5 or more yards, it had several options on second and third down. If a team gained only a few yards or the ball was thrown for a loss, it was almost forced to throw on subsequent downs.

While some teams still follow this plan, the San Diego Chargers have shown that a team can be successful with an offense that throws the ball on 80 to 90 per cent of its offensive plays. The Chargers have also been responsible for redefining the offensive positions. In conventional offenses the tight end is primarily responsible for blocking. He is bigger and stronger than most receivers and is employed as a receiver only on short passing plays or as a safety valve if other receivers are covered. Under the Chargers' system the tight end is a receiver first and a blocker second.

The intention of any pass play is to create a situation where the receiver is able to find an open area of the field. In some cases pure speed is utilized, but more likely a receiver will try to use a fake to shake off man-to-man coverage or attempt to beat a zone defense by finding an open space or "seam" between two areas of the zone.

A pattern in which the receiver uses speed to run straight down the field is called a "post pattern." If the receiver goes downfield and then cuts sharply to the sidelines, this is called a "down-and-out" pattern. If he were to run downfield and then cut into the middle of the field, it would be known as a "crossing" pattern.

A play-action pass is one in which the quarterback first fakes a handoff to one of his running backs. This move freezes the defense momentarily, often long enough for the receiver to slip beyond the coverage.

Another popular pass is the "screen" pass. On this play the offensive linemen attempt to set up a wall of blockers, and the quarterback throws to a receiver—usually one of the running backs—behind this wall. On this play the offensive linemen usually allow some of the defensive players to charge the quarterback, effectively taking them out of the play when the quarterback lobs the ball to his receiver.

There are four basic running plays, a power run inside, an off-tackle play, a draw and a sweep.

The power run is used when a team has to gain a yard or two. Teams usually employ two tight ends in this situation for maximum blocking, and the ball is carried by the fullback, who is the heaviest man in the backfield. A variation of this play is the quarterback sneak, in which the quarterback keeps the ball himself and follows the blocking of the center and the guards.

Off-tackle plays are generally run to the outside. The tackle attempts to block the defensive end or the outside linebacker to the inside, leaving a hole for the running back to go outside.

Draw plays usually go inside and are based on a delay. The quarterback will take a few steps backward, as if to pass, then hand off to the running back.

The sweep, as popularized by the late Vince Lombardi with the Green Bay Packers, is play that stresses strength and execution. In this play the running back goes wide, usually after taking a toss from the quarterback, and the linemen move in the same direction, providing him with a wall of blockers.

DEFENSE

There are any number of defensive strategies employed in professional football, but they all have the same basic intention, which is to dilute the offensive team's strength.

If the offensive team has a passing attack based on one outstanding receiver, the defense may counter by "double-teaming," assigning two defenders to that receiver. If the offensive team likes to control the play by running the ball and grinding out yardage, a defensive team might stack its defensive line and linebackers with strong players who are able to stop the run.

The defense can also take advantage of offensive weakness. If there is a weak link in the offensive line, the defense may assign its best pass rusher to play opposite that player in the hope of putting more pressure on the quarterback.

Defensive teams also take advantage of special strategies. For example, defensive backs are generally used to cover receivers downfield. But on some occasions a team may use one of its defensive backs to rush the quarterback, a tactic known as "safety blitz." Linebackers can also be used on a blitz.

There are two basic defensive formations. One is the standard 4–3, in which a team uses four defensive, or down, linemen: three linebackers and four defensive backs. This formation allows a team to put maximum pressure on the quarterback and is also effective against the run.

In recent years more teams have adopted the 3–4, or 34 defense. This defense employs three down linemen and four linebackers. There is less pressure on the quarterback and the defense is more vulnerable to the run, but the 34 does allow for better coverage of receivers in passing situations.

There are also two specialty defenses that are used exten-
sively. The first is the goal-line, or short-yardage, defense. This
defense is employed against an offense that needs only a short
gain for a touchdown or a first down. The defense is tightly
packed and usually surges towards the middle to push back any
forward charge by the offense.

The second specialty defense is the "nickel" defense (its name
is derived from the five-cent piece), used in obvious passing
situations. In this defense one of the linebackers is replaced by a
fifth defensive back, thus giving the defense an extra man for
pass coverage. The nickel defense is usually employed by a team
with a comfortable lead. It will allow an offensive team some
progress, particularly along the ground, but it guards against
some quick penetration, the kind that suddenly disfigures a nice-
looking score-board as the clock winds down.

The conclusion has to be that the objectives and the means of
football could scarcely be blunter. The game is about winning
ground, about relentless progress or lost chances. Even in the
boxing ring it is possible to yield ground, to destroy your
opponent by granting him space that he cannot use. In soccer
some of the best midfield players operate from deep in their own
half, shaping the game, striking forward only when they feel they
have removed risk. The great Dutchman Johan Cruyff once
destroyed England at Wembley, and I do not recall his crossing
the halfway line. When Germany's master sweeper Franz
Beckenbauer was signed by New York Cosmos for some outrageous sum, an executive of that club, weaned on the gridiron,
was outraged by the German's position deep in defense. The
executive became notorious in soccer circles for his declaration,
"Tell the Kraut to get his ass up front. We don't pay a million for
a guy to hang around in defense."

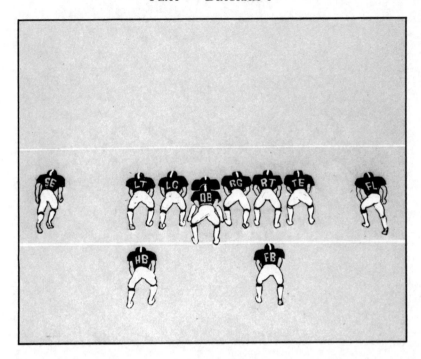

This is the basic offensive formation used by NFL teams. The offense is balanced, with two receivers, the tight end and a wide receiver, lined up on the "strong" side. As the ball is not placed in the middle of the field to start a play, the strong side is, for obvious reasons, usually the side of the field with the most room.

The formation permits a maximum of options. The quarterback can run with the ball, hand off to a halfback or fullback or throw to any of his eligible receivers (back, the tight end or either wide receiver, flanker or split end). The key to success, whatever option is chosen by the quarterback, lies in the ability of the offensive line, the unsung heroes of football, to withstand pressure from the opposing defensive line and linebackers. When the obvious objective is simply to pass, the quarterback drops back 6 yards into what is known as the "Shotgun formation."

Key: **SE**, split end; **LT**, left tackle; **LG**, left guard; **RG**, right guard; **RT**, right tackle; **TE**, tight end; **FL**, flanker; **QB**, Quarterback; **HB**, halfback; **FB**, fullback.

The "I" formation has grown in popularity over the last decade. It has the versatility of the basic offensive formation and one clear advantage.

With the fullback and the halfback lined up behind the quarterback initially, the defense is unable to make a clear decision about which back is to receive the ball in the event of a running play. The diagram shows the effect of this maneuver, with fullback blocking for the halfback or, in this case, tailback.

As always, the objective is to confuse the defensive unit and to create space.

A classic variant of the "I" formation is the "Power I," which is used in short-yardage situations when a team is close to either a first down or a touchdown. In this formation the offensive line is usually tightly packed, and a second tight end is employed in place of one of the wide receivers. This provides better blocking resources. The objective of the play is to punch the ball forward for a short distance. Most teams fake a hand-off to the first back in the "I" formation and then use that back as an additional blocker for the eventual ball carrier. Another option is for the quarterback to retain the ball.

The quarterback will seek to gain the necessary yardage behind the blocking of center and guard. This play is called a quarterback sneak.

Key: **LT**, left tackle; **LG**, left guard; **C**, center; **RG**, right guard; **FB**, fullback; **RT**, right tackle; **TE**, tight end; **TB**, tailback (halfback); **QB**, quarterback.

The "curl" is designed to maintain a team's downfield momentum rather than some spectacular game-breaking advance. The receivers, including tight end, break straight downfield, then curl off their course, in the case of the receivers toward the middle of the field.

The "curl" is used principally when the defensive backs, concerned with long penetration, begin to grant the receiving unit a cushion of space.

The "curl" will not usually win a game, but it is a relatively safe option for short-to-medium passing progress.

Key: **TE**, tight end; **FL**, flanker (wide receiver); **LT**, left tackle; **LG**, left guard; **C**, center; **RG**, right guard; **RT**, right tackle; **HB**, halfback; **FB**, fullback; **QB**, quarterback.

The "down and out" relies on the speed and elusiveness of the wide receiver and the strong arm of the quarterback.

The usual version is for the wide receiver to run downfield for 10 yards and then break toward the sideline at a 45° angle.

To shake clear of corner backs and safeties, the receiver will employ either fakes or feints or pure speed.

A variant is for the wide receiver to go downfield 10 yards, fake as if he were cutting outside, and then turn back sharply toward the quarterback so that he is in a position to come back for a short pass. This is known as a "button hook." In the above pattern the receiver on the right has gone downfield and then cut inside. This is known as the "down and in." The tight end, meanwhile, has gone down on a short route and offers himself as a safety valve in the middle seam between the deep backs and the line backers.

Key: **FL**, flanker (wide receiver); **TE**, tight end; **QB**, quarterback.

The "screen" pass is essentially an ambush of the onrushing defensive team. The quarterback drops back to pass, and his linemen put up only token opposition before allowing the defense to slip through. The running backs seek to find space behind the rush and take a pass from the quarterback. Meanwhile the offensive line reforms to provide a blocking "screen" for the ball carrier.

Key: **SE**, split end; **FL**, flanker; **LT**, left tackle; **LG**, left guard; **C**, center; **RG**, right guard; **RT**, right tackle; **HB**, halfback; **QB**, quarterback.

The "reverse" play is an elaborate feint involving the quarterback, the halfback and the flanker.

The offensive line fakes a heavy blocking rush on the right side of the line. The quarterback hands the ball off to a halfback, who makes to sweep behind the screen of blockers, then in turn hands off to the flanker, who is breaking to the left side.

The move can break open the field for the offense, but it has to be performed with precision and with some effort at disguise. If the defense has an inkling of the feint, the chance of a serious gain in yardage is slim.

Key: **SE**, split end (receiver); **LT**, left tackle; **LG**, left guard; **QB**, quarterback; **C**, center; **RT**, right tackle; **TE**, tight end; **FB**, fullback; **RG**, right guard; **HB**, halfback; **FL**, flanker (receiver).

The off-tackle offense is designed to give the running back space outside. It is aimed to penetrate to the right or left of the offensive tackles and involves the quarterback faking a hand-off to one backfield player, who goes into the line as a decoy. The quarterback then hands off the ball to the other running back, who looks for daylight between the tackle and the tight end. The frequency with which the move is used tends to be related closely to the talent of a team's backfield. The off-tackle maneuver is valuable for a team that has running backs with genuine speed and/or power.

Key: **LT**, left tackle; **LG**, left guard; **C**, center; **RG**, right guard; **RT**, right tackle; **FB**, fullback; **TE**, tight end; **TB**, tailback; **QB**, quarterback.

The "pitch-out" is a backward or lateral pass to a running back who has already achieved some momentum. It is useful in that it allows the halfback more chance of penetration. it requires some care from the quarterback, who has to time the placement of the pass perfectly as the receiver accelerates.

Key: **FS**, free safety; **SE**, split end; **SS**, strong safety; **LB**, linebacker; **LT**, left tackle; **QB**, quarterback; **C**, center; **LG**, left guard; **RT**, right tackle; **TE**, tight end; **RG**, right guard; **TB**, tailback (halfback); **FB**, fullback.

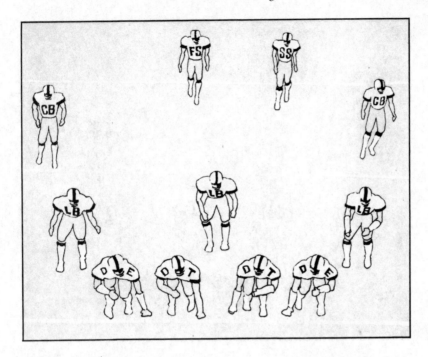

The NFL's basic defensive formation is the conventional 4–3 stance on the line of scrimmage. It has a four-man defensive line, with three linebackers deployed behind and four defensive backs.

The defensive line's responsibility is to put pressure on the quarterbacks and to make the initial stop on running plays.

The linebackers are concerned primarily with following up on running coverage but also have responsibility for short passing patterns. The defensive backs must cover downfield passing patterns and be prepared to adjust for penetrating running plays.

Key: **DE**, defensive end; **DT**, defensive tackle; **LB**, linebacker; **CB**, corner back; **FS**, free safety; **SS**, strong safety.

The 3–4 defensive formation is a reaction to the rapid growth of the passing game. In this formation just three linemen are deployed for rushing duties, and an extra linebacker is inserted to help with pass coverage.

This variation certainly offers more security against the pass, but it is not without risk. The set-up is vulnerable to a powerful running performance from the opposition, and it puts a much greater workload on the rushing lineman.

Key: **DE**, defensive end; **NG**, nose guard; **LB**, linebacker; **CB**, corner back; **FS**, free safety; **SS**, strong safety.

4

The Run to Daylight

To the virgin eye what American football needs above all is a point of focus, a key from which understanding can flow naturally. This is probably more true of football than of any other team game. Soccer can be chaotic, but its chaos is readily assimilated. There is an obvious unity about each team; a right fullback brings the ball out of defense, shapes to pass the ball inside, and every outfield player responds to the emphasis of his body. By comparison football can be utterly obscure. It is, for instance, the only team game in which certain players can have wonderful seasons, be the darlings of the crowd and yet never get their hands on the ball. This is the likelihood for the men on the line who block and protect, who wrestle and grunt in pursuit of inches of ground and fractions of seconds. The linemen operate in one of the half-dozen sub-plots which spring to life each time the center releases the ball to the quarterback. On which sub-plot do you focus? Do you watch the quarterback stepping into a pocket of cover, arm poised for the pass, weighing his options, or, if the offense unravels, scrambling downfield, gingerly as a thoroughbred negotiating a street filled with traffic? Do you watch the linebackers, eyes hard, mouths foaming, as they tear into the blitz, or the corner backs shuffling to anticipate the flight path of some bomb that might explode around their heads if the receiver is given enough ground, enough time? I don't think so. I think for your sense of the classic shape of this game, you look to the running back. You have to focus on him as you would an infantryman if you really needed to know about the essence of war.

TOUGH GOING

The running back is central to a football team. Games can be won on the pass—many of them are in the modern NFL—but going into action without belief in your backfield, your ability to generate impact along the ground, is to go to sea without a rudder. A good running back has to be physically brave and resilient beyond reason. He takes more punishment than any other player. His knees are attacked relentlessly by the linebackers. The running back can also be called up to block, has to build the kind of momentum that can throw off-balance some of the biggest, most obdurate men in professional sport. He also has to punch in touchdowns when a team has slogged downfield in one of those wars of attrition that develop when action in the air is abandoned for one reason or another. Ask any old infantryman and he will tell you, with a mixture of pique and pride, that when all else failed, when there was fog in the sky and mud on the ground, they sent in the ground troops. So it is with the running back. He knows that he is abused, and if he is at all reflective, he will conclude that he is doing things for which the hinges of the human body were simply not designed, especially on the unyielding, skin-burning surface of artificial grass. Yet game in, game out, he does his duty, follows the solemn exhortation of the most demanding of coaches, Vince Lombardi, which was: "Run to daylight." He takes the shots at his knees, the hits that send all breath shooting from his body so that for a while he is lifeless on the ground, and then, when he senses he has made his last "carry" of the day, he pulls off his helmet and perhaps gives a small bow to the crowd. The spectators cheer wildly because to them the running back is always the man to celebrate above all. The essence of his game is contact, whether it is frontal or from some sidelong swipe, and this too is the essence of football. You think of running backs when you hear the old saying of Notre Dame coach Knute Rockne: "When the going gets tough, the tough get going."

For the running back there are twin peaks, those of pain and of glory. I recall a summer's day in 1981 in North Dallas, Texas, a day of overwhelming heat. I went to the practice field of the Dallas Cowboys. Training camp had yet to open, but many of the veteran players had reported early to the club's conditioning coach, a huge ex-US Marine named Bob Ward. He was putting the veterans through a series of weight exercises. The workplace, under a roof of corrugated iron, was at the edge of the practice field that was shut off from the world by a high fence of blue. The sky was also a vast blue in sharp contrast to red, burned faces. The workplace was awash with sweat. Thousands of dollars' worth of equipment cluttered the compound and spilled out on to the field. On a wall there was a notice in large, stark lettering. It said, "Football is the most violent of all games. In no other sport is bodily contact so pronounced, explosive power put to such repeated use and total body power of such importance." I had gone to see Tony Dorsett, one of the great modern running backs. Dorsett was not obliged to be at this early work, to have his every move monitored by this former Marine with the crew cut who seemed a little hurt when I suggested that he might have enjoyed an executive job in the Spanish Inquisition. But then Dorsett was candid enough about his imperatives. He told me, "I know that each year the pressure gets worse in this game. Every year the kids are coming through bigger and faster. You look at them at training camp [the Cowboys would be starting their camp in a week's time], and you say, man, where will this end? I've come early because I want to be in the best possible shape for camp and for the new season. I want people to know that Tony Dorsett is ready. I don't want to encourage anybody."

For all his reputation, Dorsett's concern was easy enough to understand. He was known for racy living, and though his first three seasons in the NFL had been spectacular—he had gained more than 1,000 yards in each—his somewhat flashy personality was deeply at odds with the style of Cowboys coach Tom Landry, a dour Texan who, midway through the previous season, had fired his brilliant linebacker Hollywood Henderson for "disciplinary reasons." Henderson also had a free lifestyle, but his real downfall came when he smiled and waved at the television cameras in the depth of a Dallas defeat. It was thus a good time for Dorsett, a graduate of the University of Pittsburgh team, to make a statement about his commitment to football in general and Dallas Cowboys in particular. Dorsett had already taken much physical punishment when I spoke to him that steamy Texas day. "I've become a lot more serious about my life in the last couple of years," said Dorsett. "I'm doing this work because I need it to stay ahead. In football you just can't stand still. If you do, they come along and eat you up. There was a time when I feared that you could burn up your body too quickly. Now I feel more confident when I'm working, stretching. I've come to the point when I think the pain is good. It makes you feel you are really doing something."

"The pain is good": it might be some kind of crazy justification, an attempt to give meaning to the playing of a position

where the pain is implicit, where the weeks between high
summer and January are a series of journeys to physical limits
and then recovery to further challenges.

RUNNING OUT OF THE LIMELIGHT

Dorsett was investigated for cocaine possession in the summer of
1983, a week before the start of another training camp, another
journey up to the front-line trenches. He became another
statistic in the growing story of professional football players and
drug dependency. Some saw him as another example of a highly
paid athlete with too much time and money on his hands. Others
argued that a Tony Dorsett was subject to unreasonable
pressures, that sooner or later something, perhaps a part of his
body, maybe a corner of his mind, was bound to give.

Chuck Muncie of the San Diego Chargers is another modern
running back who has been caught in the spread of drugs.
Despite his great speed, and a powerful body (6 feet 3 inches, 217
pounds) there were signs that Muncie was tiring of the conflict
before he moved to San Diego from the hapless New Orleans
Saints. By 1980 the Saints had become so bad, so devoid of all
the basic strengths of a football team, that the fans had taken to
turning up at the Superdrome wearing over their heads paper
bags in which they had cut eye-holes. They explained that they
didn't want to be seen on national television as fans of the
world's worst team. But however inept the team, however
marked its inability to clear a route for a running back, Muncie
was under contract and obliged to tuck the ball under his arm
and make the run for daylight. He sensed—most acutely when
he lay in his bed after a game, his body a latticework of bruises—
that he was really running into the night, that whatever he
achieved personally would be lost in some wider futility. He had
to fight the hardest battle in football without any real support.
His move to San Diego, a team that puts so much emphasis on
aerial offense that it is known as Air Coryell after coach Don
Coryell, was nothing so much as a liberation.

Great running backs have a tendency to finish up with poor or
mediocre teams, who, under a system aimed at equalizing
strength through the League, get first pick of the best of the
talent emerging from the college game. Sometimes struggling

clubs trade away their choices in the annual draft in favor of more immeditae help, and thus a Dorsett may find himself with a club as powerful as the Cowboys. But there are many more stories of truly gifted running backs attempting, almost single-handedly, to lift the fortunes of desperate clubs. Muncie is one example. The immensely strong Earl Campbell of the Houston Oilers is another.

In the early 1980s Campbell's reputation had become almost mythical. Known as the Tyler Rose, after his birthplace in Texas, Campbell's ability to overwhelm defenses persuaded some that he could become the greatest running back of all time. At 5 feet 11 inches and weighing 224 pounds, Campbell came into the League in 1978 with the impact of a heavy tank. He had won the Heisman Trophy for the nation's best college player, and his ability to evade or power through tackles had had the professional scouts more excited than at any time since the explosion of O. J. Simpson a decade earlier. But again there was the spectacle of a fine young talent being hit by teams of tacklers who seemed to stop short only at the employment of a breaking ball as they sought its demolition. Inevitably, Campbell began to complain about the frustrations of fighting a lost cause. His coach, the amusing Bum Phillips, who wears a stetson and enjoys off-color country and western jokes, was fired as Houston attempted to placate their superstar and build a competitive side. But such construction takes time, certainly no less than two years, and two years can represent 50 per cent of the professional careers of many running backs. Campbell was tied to a contract, and he had to accept that he had no real alternative but to soldier on, battle in the trenches and hope that his body would hold out long enough for him to glimpse the light that shines beyond failure.

Walter Payton of the Chicago Bears has long been operating on this principle. At 5 feet 11 inches and 203 pounds, Payton is no tank, but his ability to thread his way through a defense, his capacity to absorb punishment, has earned him a $2 million contract. Before the 1982 season *Sports Illustrated* ran a cover story on Payton, entitled "Chicago's One-Man Gang." But then Payton, who joined Chicago from the modest Jackson State University in Mississippi, has also shown his frustration. After physical maulings in the 1980 season he simmered to the point of open rebellion, complaining after one game against Detroit, "I couldn't raise my hand over my head. They threw three or four passes to me and I just couldn't get my arms up to catch them." Chicago seemed to be on the point of disintegration, their ability to win space just about nil. Payton, resilient and tricky, had always been willing to do his share of the punishing work, but increasingly he found it difficult to see a future beyond the bruises and the pain. After a game with Tampa Bay he said, "It got to the point where there wasn't any place to go. I attacked the defense: as a result of that, I had guys who were trying to tackle me lying on the ground. I broke my shoulder pads." At the end of an earlier, more promising season Payton had given gifts of wristwatches to his teammates on the offensive line. It is a common enough gesture in football, where one man's physical and professional survival can often depend on the work of teammates out of the spectator's eye and the television frame. But in 1980 Payton felt no compulsion to make such a gesture. Instead he told a reporter, "This year I'll give 'em pieces of my body."

Payton had to be compensated. Remove him from the Bears, and a club that had once been the nation's most powerful would be a loser without redemption, a team as wretched as New Orleans or the fast-sliding Baltimore Colts. Owner George Halas, fighting his life-long conservative instincts, eventually gave Payton his $2 million contract, which was one of the most lucrative in the game. From Halas it was a concession that he needed the spirit and the talent of a young black who had grown up poor and desperately ambitious in the back country of Mississippi. For the breed of running backs it was rare evidence that their short, punishing careers need not always end in pain and disillusion.

THE OLD SCHOOL: NEVERS, A FLAWLESS PLAYER

Jim Thorpe and Red Grange were more than running backs. They threw and kicked as well as ran, and they belonged to an altogether different age, when diet and training and scientific weight work had not produced huge men who could cover 40 yards in only slightly more than four seconds and who would submit to extraordinary levels of discipline (some might even say mind-programming). Thorpe and Grange played a game that didn't drive them into narrow lanes. However, great as they were, one school of thought says that neither of them ever exploited this freedom quite as well as Ernie Nevers.

Nevers, like Thorpe and Grange, could do a lot more than simply run with the ball. He could pass long and short, send wicked punts spiraling through the wind, and when he kicked for goal he had both vast distance and an accuracy that sometimes seemed uncanny. It was said that playing against Nevers was an exercise in futility. Stop him in the air and he would come at you along the ground. A tall, handsome man, his athletic ability was informed by a sharp intelligence. He made his name at Stanford University near San Francisco, an institution that has always prided itself on its academic prowess, even among its athletes, of whom tennis's *enfant terrrible* John McEnroe is perhaps one of the least likely. Nevers's coach at Stanford, the famous Pop Warner, said that he was the football player of his dreams. "Nevers is without a flaw," said Warner in an extraordinary speech for a football coach.

The point was confirmed in 1929, when Nevers led his Chicago Cardinals to a 40–6 points victory over the Chicago Bears. Nevers scored all of the Cardinals' points: he scored six touchdowns, added four conversions. It was one of those performances that occasionally erupt in the greatest of athletes. But America had been given notice.

After leading Stanford to the prestigious Rose Bowl game in Pasadena, Nevers had been signed by the Duluth Eskimos for $25,000. The Eskimos, who would eventually become the Chicago Cardinals, exploited Nevers as relentlessly as George Halas and the Bears had Grange. The Eskimos left Minnesota in September and did not return until January. And it seems that the club, having parted with $25,000, was reluctant to spend anything more on its great talent. George Sullivan reports that the Eskimos refused to supply Nevers with all the tape he required to protect his body before games. Sometimes he would cover himself with the thick black tape used by electricians. It is perhaps another small example of the psychology of the running back. Ultimately, even someone as gifted as Nevers had to deal with his own wounds.

Nevers played his last game in 1931. His pro career had lasted five years and though they were lucrative by the standards of those days, and especially when set against the bleak background of the collapse of Wall Street, it has to be said that every cent was repaid, both at the box office and in terms of the unnatural demands made on a man's body. Nevers would always have the legacy of his football days, the arthritis in the joints, the twinges which came with the first hint of winter. It was the classic experience of a running back.

THE JUICE: A BEAUTIFUL BLACK CAT

O. J. Simpson's was another kind of story. He was christened Orenthal James Simpson, but soon enough he was known simply as O.J. or The Juice. He was sleek and quick at 6 feet 1 inch, 220 pounds, and when he came out of the University of Southern California in 1968 the professional scouts said that here might be the ultimate running back. He didn't invite punishment; he didn't believe that his job was to smash his body relentlessly against the walls of defense. He had electric speed; he ran with a wonderful smoothness; and he moved his feet, feinting, bursting, like the very best welterweights. He had grown up in the California of the Beach Boys. To O.J. the best vibrations came from grace and wit; running backs might be categorized by many as bulldogs, but he was a cat, a beautiful black cat.

From time to time you see O.J. at some star-spangled occasion, perhaps a big fight in Las Vegas or a football game or a movie premiere. O.J. flashes a brilliant smile at the cameras, shakes hands with the exuberance of someone with plenty of reasons to feel secure. His face is seen regularly on television commercials. In 1983 he made his debut as a television sports commentator. There will always be something for The Juice.

In his final year at Southern Cal he won the Heisman Trophy for the best college football player. In the Rose Bowl game he thrilled the huge crowd with his raking runs. O.J., it was already clear, was a gift to the game, one of those individuals who inevitably sets new standards, defines style and ability all over again. But for the draft of college players, Simpson would have been plucked by one of the great clubs. Instead the call came from Buffalo. For O. J. Simpson, Buffalo, scarred and crumbling on the cold lakeshore, might have been situated on another planet. I remember calling a newspaper colleague in Buffalo from a nearby town and suggesting a meeting. "Fine," he said,

1 Archie Manning—a brave and resourceful quarterback for whom life in the pros has mostly been a battle against heavy odds. Here Los Angeles Rams defensive end Fred Dryer bears down on Manning as he seeks an uncovered New Orleans Saints receiver. In this game New Orleans receivers were mostly covered and Manning took another physical beating. The Saints lost by 27 points to 7. New Orleans traded Manning to Houston Oilers in 1982. It was no rest cure. Manning had to perform behind another inept offensive line and it was some relief when he was traded again, this time to Minnesota, in the fall of 1983.

2 (top left) Tony Dorsett (33) makes a typical thrusting probe on behalf of Dallas Cowboys as team-mate Billy Joe Dupree provides a blocking screen against the attention of Green Bay Packers' linebacker John Anderson. **3** (bottom left) at the line of scrimmage, the fierce Jack Youngblood (85) leads the defensive unit of Los Angeles Rams against bitter rivals Los Angeles Raiders. **4** (above) Pittsburgh's masterful quarterback Terry Bradshaw (12) is less phlegmatic than usual as he comes under heavy pressure from Cincinnati Bengal defensive star Ross Browner.

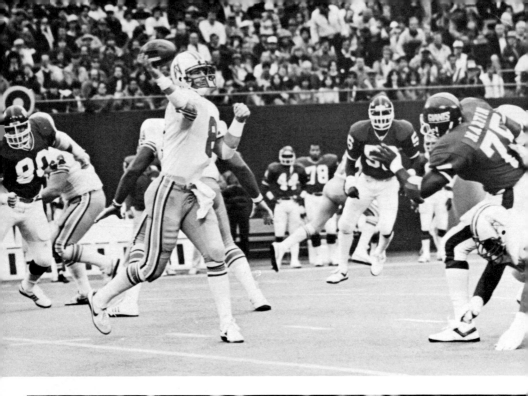

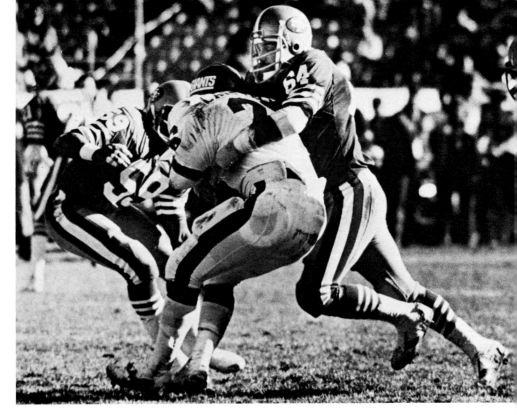

5 (top left) For Manning, there is always pressure. Manning is encircled by New York Giants as the Houston Oilers offensive line crumbles. For the Giants, defensive ends George Martin (75) and Phil Tabor (80) apply most pressure as the excellent linebacker Lawrence Taylor (56) also moves in. **6** (bottom left) San Francisco linebackers Jack 'Hacksaw' Reynolds (64) and Willie Harper (59) arrest the progress of New York Giants' running back Rob Carpenter (26). **7** (above) Ken 'The Snake' Stabler is a quarterback of panache and ingenuity, and in 1983 there were signs that he might lead New Orleans away from the Basin Street Blues.

8 Walter Payton, Chicago's 'one man gang'. Quick, durable, brave, Payton in many games takes
on almost the entire offensive burden of the Chicago Bears. In a good year he gave presents of gold
watches to his protectors on the offensive line. In a less happy year he said bitterly, "Maybe this
time I'll give them bits of my body." For a while Payton hinted that he wanted to leave Chicago
but the Bears came in with a huge contract for the man from Mississippi. Here he shows his heels
to Cleveland Browns' linebacker Clayton Matthews.

9 Mean Joe Greene (75) leads the Pittsburgh "breaking" squad. In the company of team-mate L.C. Greenwood (68), defensive tackle Greene overwhelms Cincinnati's tackle Tony Munoz (77). Greene made a fortune in television soft drink ads. He played an amiable giant. On the field he was noted more for his ability to generate pure hostility. Greene was a cornerstone of the Steeler dynasty built by Chuck Noll, the dominating coach of the late 70s. Of Greene, Noll says "You could always be sure about Joe. You always knew what you'd get. It would always be the real stuff."

10 Some say there'll never be another Jim Brown. He stood 6 foot 2 inches tall, weighed 230 lbs, and was the purest of locomotion. One opponent described what it was like to confront the great running back of the Cleveland Browns, who was installed in the Pro Football Hall of Fame in 1971. Willie Davis of the Green Bay Packers said "I hit him, I hit him good, and we both went down. It was one of the few times in my life when my whole body was aching. Only my pride made me get up." Brown shattered records at the University of Syracuse, from which he graduated in 1956. In nine years of action for the Browns, he broke eight rushing and scoring records in the NFL. In 1983, when those records came under pressure from Pittsburgh's Franco Harris, Brown discussed the possibility of making a return to the game. He was 43 years old. He was one of the most gifted individuals ever to play the game. Nor did he lack a healthy ego.

11 (above left) Jim Thorpe was elected to be the first president of the NFL in 1920, but it was as a player that he gave extraordinary momentum to professional football. Those who claim that Jim Brown was the greatest player of all time inevitably meet fierce resistance from supporters of Thorpe. He won gold medals in the 1912 Olympics in Stockholm, and when King Gustav V made the presentation he said "You are the greatest athlete in the world." Thorpe said "Thanks, King." **12** (above right) O.J. Simpson—The Juice. Simpson is a successful television commentator now but he will always be known as the magical runner of the Buffalo Bills. Brown and Thorpe were physically superb specimens who mastered the game. Simpson was one of its ultimate artists.

13 (above) Johnny Unitas of the Baltimore Colts had none of the glamour of the big-name quarterbacks. He was, as he played, undemonstrative, functional, always professional. It seemed that he would never make it in the big league. He drifted into sandlot football, another dreamer hoping to hear the call. He heard it and many students of the game say that no-one understood better the particular demands of his job. It was said that Joe Namath would always thrill the crowd and Johnny Unitas would always get the job done.

14 (right) Tony Dorsett . . . the action of a thoroughbred.

15 (left) Ken Stabler, on duty for Oakland before they moved south and became the Los Angeles Raiders, throws a bomb as San Diego defensive end Leroy Jones moves in for the hit. Stabler has two of the great qualities of the natural quarterback: he is patient and can absorb a hit. **16** (above) Walter Payton eats up ground for Chicago, team-mate Noah Jackson (65) having created an opening. It was another fruitful day for Payton against the Washington Redskins. He covered 107 yards in 17 rushes and the Bears whipped the Redskins 35 points to 21.

17 Mark Gastineau (99) is one of the most controversial players in the NFL. He is a fiery defensive end for the New York Jets but purists deplore his habit of performing elaborate dances whenever he hits his quarterback. Here, he attempts something less spectacular but just as vital to his team. He seeks to steal the ball from Miami quarterback David Woodley.

18 (top left) Y.A. 'Yelverton Abraham' Tittle has said, "Kids in my part of Texas would rather play football than eat." He played the game so well that he could eat in the best restaurants throughout his quarterbacking career. **19** (top right) George Halas was known as 'Papa Bear' for his building of the Chicago Bears. A great player, an incisive coach, and a tough administrator, Halas helped shape the league from its first meeting in a Canton, Ohio car sales room to the glory days of Super Bowls and billion-dollar television contracts. **20** (above left) Vince Lombardi made Green Bay Packers one of the great teams in the history of American football. In the process, some said, he influenced the way Americans thought. He insisted that "Winning wasn't the important thing . . . it was the only thing." **21** (above right) Ernie Nevers had it all. He could kick the ball huge distances and run like the wind, and his old coach Pop Warner said that he was "A flawless football player."

DO YOU REMEMBER?

22 (above) More pressure for Archie Manning in the service of the downtrodden New Orleans Saints. Manning, who never had enough time or cover in New Orleans, attempts to fire a pass beyond the rush of Los Angeles Rams. **23** (left) Harold 'Red' Grange inspired much purple prose in the 1920s, not least from the celebrated sports writer Grantland Rice, who wrote of him thus: "a streak of fire, a breath of flame; eluding all who reach and clutch; a grey ghost thrown into the game, that rival hands may rarely touch . . ." Grange brought a new dimension to the professional game when he signed professional forms for the Chicago Bears in 1925 after a career of spectacular achievement with the University of Illinois. **24** (top right) Walter Payton (34) breaks through the defensive line of the Kansas City Chiefs. **25** (bottom right) John Schumacher (62) has carved some space against the San Francisco defense and his Houston colleague, running back Earl Campbell—the Tyler Rose—makes the dart for daylight.

26 This is the kind of confrontation which makes American football compulsive television for the world's most powerful nation. Tony Dorsett of the Dallas Cowboys has breached the wall of the Pittsburgh Steelers, but not completely, and the price for his audacity will be heavy—temporary burial by Mean Joe Greene (75).

"but don't drive here. I'll come over to see you. All we could do
here is have a beer and watch a building decay." There are many
such jokes about Buffalo, but O. J. Simpson was hard put to
smile in 1968. Not only was Buffalo an affront to Simpson's West
Coast lifestyle, but its football club, the Bills, was for four years a
serious threat to his health.

Talent was spread thin in Buffalo, and it was grimly evident
that Simpson's contribution had to be much more far-reaching
than that of a superbly gifted running back. He had to operate
also as a receiver, an altogether different art in the modern game.
Occasionally, he was even involved in the suicide alley of
"special teams." It was the kind of physical pressure that could
have obliterated the talent of O. J. Simpson, and he recalls,
"Those first years in Buffalo were very hard; after the years in
California I began to forget how it was playing winning football.
I realized I just had to tough it out. I had a contract. What could
I do?"

Relief came in 1971. Buffalo appointed a new coach who
realized that Simpson was a prime asset that was being allowed
to dwindle. It was as though the Buffalo Bills had a classic colt
harnessed to a plough. The new coach, Lou Saban, made moves
to improve the club's blocking potential, signing up players who
could clear space for the elegant stride of Simpson. In 1973
Saban's policy produced one of the single richest harvests in
professional football history. The Juice, the thoroughbred in the
white suit bearing the number 32, became the man he had
always promised to be in the Californian sunshine.

The records simply evaporated in the heat of Simpson's 1973.
If a running back has gained 1,000 yards in an NFL season, he
has had an excellent year; his body has held together, and his
appetite for punishment has not been exhausted. In 1973
Simpson ran for more than 2,000 yards. To be precise, he
achieved 2,003 yards. He did it in short, searing bursts; he did it
in tricky, mazy patterns and in lovely clean breaks. Simpson
could produce instant momentum, and beyond the speed there
was an instinct for the light, a subliminal sense of where the
defensive cover had become frayed and vulnerable. He knew
where, precisely, to strike.

In one game his achievement was astounding. He covered
250 yards. No one had ever run 250 yards in a game before,
not Grange, not Thorpe, not Nevers. It was the triumphant

statement of a man who had emerged from bad days, who had bitten on all his frustrations and taken his chance when it came, finally. Simpson credits much of his liberation to the arrival in Buffalo of the fine blocker, offensive lineman Reggie McKenzie. Says Simpson, "When Reggie came to Buffalo we were floundering with guys well past their prime or guys that would never reach it. When I was a little down Reggie would always lift me up. One day I said we could shoot for the target of 1,500 yards and he said, 'No, Juice, let's shoot for 2,000.'"

Simpson ran past the 2,000-yard mark in the last game of the season. It was a raw day out at Shea Stadium in Queens, New York. The New York Jets were shoved to one side by the massive forearms of McKenzie, and Simpson, keeping his feet magically on the snow-covered field, set a record that would stand for all time. Simpson had accomplished his 2,000 yards in a fourteen-game season. Now, as a result of expansion, the NFL plays a sixteen-game regular season.

There were other records in 1973: most rushing attempts in a season (332), most in one game (39), most games with more than 200 yards gained (3), and most games with more than 100 yards gained (11). The statistics, even the most dazzling of them, are dry enough. The reality was a wonderfully liquid grace. "O.J., O.J., Juice, Juice," the crowds chanted, confidently, expectantly. Football is a harsh game, and sometimes it descended to outright brutality, but O.J. carried the game and the fans above that.

Once he explained that he had patterned his game on Gale Sayers and Hugh McIlhenny. Runners of artistry for the Chicago Bears and the San Francisco 49ers, Sayers and McIlhenny had not found it necessary to prove themselves in primeval collisions; they saw themselves as elusive men of speed who had the gift to outrun and outwit any defense. *The Complete Handbook of Pro Football* says of Sayers, "sleek as a greyhound, fluid as a panther, deceptive as a wildcat." If this sounds a trifle extravagant, there is no shortage of supporting evidence, not least from the members of the 1965 San Francisco team. Sayers ran in six touchdowns against the 49ers, side-stepping, feinting, driving the line. McIlhenny was willing to battle for a yard or two, but essentially he was of Sayers's school. In a game against the Dallas Texans he broke free for runs of 89 and 82 yards.

These, then, were the models for O. J. Simpson. They were the stylists who brought sunlight to the trenches, who said that there was more to the game than a series of bad accidents. Their view was in direct conflict with the thinking of Larry Csonka.

CSONKA: SHAKING THE OWLS FROM THE TREES
WITH A SCOWL

If Simpson and Sayers and McIlhenny were the refinements of football, Csonka was its crude resource. Csonka was power, unrestrained, untouched by a second thought. He grew up in Ohio farmland and became an immediate success at the University of Syracuse, NY, from where the Miami Dolphins drafted him in 1968.

Among the pros Csonka's power remained devastating. Fifteen years later, when he was employed by the Jacksonville Bulls, a USFL club, a columnist sympathized with Csonka for his inability to perform in the USFL as a recruiter as he had done in the NFL as a player. Phil Musick of *USA Today* wrote, "If only he could dip his head and ram them in the gut with his helmet, or smash them with thighs which looked as if limbs should be growing out of them, or maybe just scare them with a scowl which could shake owls from the trees." It was true, Csonka came from the most basic school of all.

His style was so primitive that there were fears that he would inflict brain damage on himself, acquire the punch-drunk wobbles of a club fighter. In his early days at Miami he suffered from almost continuous headaches. It was pointed out to him that this might have much to do with his habit of ramming the opposition with his head. Eventually, he modified his style, made more use of his beefy forearms, but he always insisted that the headaches went away only when the club acquired more efficient offensive linemen.

Csonka's finest hour came in Houston's Astrodrome in 1974. The occasion was Super Bowl VII. Csonka gave the Dolphins absolute control over the Minnesota Vikings. He was given the ball thirty-three times and gained 145 yards. Twice he rampaged over the Minnesota line for touchdowns. Miami won by 24 points to 7. For a time Csonka restated the most basic elements of football, as Riggins would do on behalf of Washington Redskins at Pasadena in 1982. He would have been perfectly at home in those early games in his native Ohio, battling with a Jim

Thorpe or a Willie Heston, bone on bone, will against will.

If Csonka had predecessors in the way that McIlhenny and Sayers were models for Simpson, they were, less precisely, Jim Taylor of the Green Bay Packers and Jim Brown of the Cleveland Browns.

Some still argue that Brown was in fact the greatest of all time, more relentless than Sayers and McIlhenny and even Simpson, more gifted than Taylor. The Green Bay rusher, a key element in the great Lombardi's empire building in the small town near Milwaukee, had one major misfortune. It was Jim Brown, who came out of the University of Syracuse with astonishing power and maturity.

There was much anger in Brown. He was black and born in Georgia, growing up in Long Island in that time of special awakening for his race. In his native south there were riots and billy clubs because blacks sought to register as voters, ride in white seats on buses, enroll in universities. But on the football field no one could put down a Jim Brown. Later he would play the part of a liberated slave in a Hollywood movie, to patchy reviews, but for his performances on the field the notices were always raves. He was 6 feet 2 inches tall, 231 pounds, when he graduated from Syracuse, where he had also played a superb game of lacrosse. He was voted the NFL's outstanding new-comer. Today he stands atop the list of all-time rushing with a total of 12,312 yards. In nine years Brown carried the ball 2,359 times for an average of 5.2 yards. These are figures that may one day be surpassed by Payton, Dorsett, Campbell or Pittsburgh's Franco Harris, but it is doubtful if the intensity of Brown's performance will ever be matched.

Indeed, the most threatening of Brown's challengers, Harris, is dogged by a criticism extraordinary in his line of work. Some whisper that there is a question mark against Harris's physical courage. When you look at the man in his Steelers uniform, the charge seems absurd. He has magnificent bearing and a face sculpted around fierce dark eyes and a large aquiline nose. The son of a black US Army man and an Italian woman, he has a bushy black beard and would make, physically at least, a glorious Othello. As he went into his twelfth NFL season in the summer of 1983—an astonishing feat of endurance in itself—he took with him an intriguing mixture of grace and raw strength and what might be described as controlled circumspection.

At times he has made a rare confession for a football player. He has admitted to some fear; he has acknowledged that mingled with the euphoria of a victory has been the aftertaste of deep apprehension. After making his first significant run in NFL football, Harris said, "All of a sudden I saw a hole, cut through it and saw these two big fellas coming after me. I was scared. I burst out fast, and the next thing I knew I was 10 yards downfield. I don't like to get hit."

More than a decade later Harris is just as honest, and nowhere more so than on the field. Often he will make his run, gain the ground he believes possible, then step neatly out of bounds before some fierce linebacker has the chance to hit gratuitously and hard. His physical candor is quite startling in the macho world of pro football. Outside that closed world, perhaps the surprise is that it should be remarkable when a man takes a logical step to preserve his health.

Harris has one foot in the tradition of selfless battling against heavy odds, another in the modern concept of weighing your chances and coming out of any situation ahead of the game, or at least physically whole. Such notions were utterly foreign to Thorpe and Grange and the formidable Joe Perry of the San Francisco 49ers, as they may be to young George Rogers of the New Orleans Saints, who recently declared, "My ambition is to run 1,500 or 2,000 yards in a season, or whatever comes first." But Rogers may be a throwback, an isolated reversion to the old way. When Campbell and Payton and Dorsett are gone, running backs may lean more toward the philosophy of Marcus Allen, the dashing young star of the Los Angeles Raiders. O. J. Simpson recently reported that Allen appeared at his apartment at 4 a.m. accompanied by four beautiful women. "I call him Mr Vanity," said The Juice, perhaps a little wistfully.

Simpson's rewards after football have been enough to keep at bay the bitterness that can taint even the greatest of careers. It is not so with Billy Cannon. Cannon is the running back who lost his way. Cannon was a fierce running back for Louisiana State University in the late 1950s before joining the Houston Oilers. He once bared his soul, told of the emotions he had experienced while playing a game at Pittsburgh: "That stadium had the worst field I ever played on. Did you know they tried that same turf on a racetrack in Florida? After about seven days they spread sand all over it. Do you know why? They were afraid the turf would ruin some $90,000 horse. The owners don't worry as much about football players because 200 more come along each year, bigger than ever.

"Boy, I remember that game. It was raining, cold. I was as sick as a dog. And I looked way up above at the people watching from the stadium club. I could see chandeliers. The people up there were eating Châteaubriand, and here I was, cold, wet and sick. I know one thing for sure. They wouldn't treat a $90,000 horse that way."

In 1983 Cannon was due to be inducted into college football's Hall of Fame as his reward for those dazzling runs for Louisiana State. But in July 1983 there came a curt statement from Vincent Draddy, board chairman of the National Football Foundation. Cannon would not be inducted. It turned out that he had just pleaded guilty to possession of millions of dollars' worth of counterfeit bank notes. When Cannon left college he was promised a chain of service stations by the oil-rich owner of the Houston club. The service stations never materialized. Perhaps it was this, or playing on bad turf while sick in Pittsburgh, or taking too many shots for too little reward for too long, that pushed Billy Cannon out of bounds, another casualty on the run to daylight.

One thing is certain. For the running back there are many degrees of success and failure between arthritis and having your picture hung in the Hall of Fame.

5

Golden Warriors

For a few days in the summer of 1983 John Elway, a tall, blond, young Californian became a perfect symbol of American success. His face, well made if a little bland, stared out from newspapers and television screens. He was on morning talk shows and late-night chats—though not too late because that would have been bad for the image.

Millions of fathers felt pangs of envy for the boy's father Jack, a football coach at San José State University. It was clear Jack Elway had given life to an American dream. His son was certain to be the first pick in the annual draft of college players by NFL clubs. He was also an excellent student at Stanford University, which requires more than a nominal presence in the classroom from its best athletes. Furthermore, and this was where the story became bizarre—almost too much—he was wanted for his baseball ability by the New York Yankees.

John Elway had America by the tail. He was also a quarterback.

Quarterback is the all-purpose American dream. The prettiest cheerleader tends to gravitate to the quarterback. Quarterbacks must have the right American stuff. It's a great help if you happen to look like John Elway. Quarterbacks have to display leadership, and there is a tendency for them to be handsome and, in the NFL, white. Quarterbacks run a football game, if only by proxy. If a running back powers through for a touchdown, or a receiver scuttles from his coverage and takes a catch, it at least appears to have been at the discretion of the quarterback. It may be that the quarterback is often little more than a glorified errand boy with a strong arm and a resilient body. He accepts the decisions of the coach, who sends in the plays. Often he becomes a kind of robot, a memory bank in which various buttons are pushed: run the ball, throw it screen pass, postpattern, sweep, draw play. . . . But if he is very good, very instinctive about the game, he can grow in authority. He can achieve freedom and a status that is hard to convey to a non-American.

On a recent space adventure Mission Control in Houston likened one of the more difficult maneuvers to "throwing a bomb [long pass] while wearing a blindfold." The assumption was implicit. Nothing, not even riding space, is beyond a good American quarterback.

Young Elway was not slow to grasp his special place in the nation's folklore. He revealed that the Yankees, the richest and most famous club in baseball, had offered him a contract worth millions of dollars despite the fact that he had not played beyond the Minor League level. It was also revealed that one Yankee scout had voiced the opinion that Elway could be the club's greatest slugger since Joe Di Maggio. The handsome Di Maggio had married Marilyn Monroe, who said to him when she returned from a tour of GI camps in Korea, "Joe, you never heard cheering like it," and Di Maggio, kissing her cheek, replied softly, "Yes, I did."

The hard edge to the Elway story was that he had made it clear he would refuse to join Baltimore Colts should they draft him. Baltimore, the weakest team in the NFL, had first choice but little chance of actually signing one of the most mature quarterbacks ever to emerge from the college game. According to Elway, one of the major disadvantages of Baltimore was the city's winter climate. He said that he had played all his football in California and didn't relish the idea of adapting to a cold climate. If Baltimore pressed, he would simply take up one of several options, including the Yankees and possibly a move to the fledgling USFL.

Baltimore's owner is a stubborn, very rich man named Robert Irsay. Within football he does not enjoy a great reputation for wisdom, and it was scarcely helped before the 1982 season when he hired as his coach Frank Kush. In 1981 Kush had found himself in a civil court. One of his former players at the University of Arizona sued him for damages, charging that coaching methods for the Sun Devils team had been inhumane. The player claimed that Kush had slapped him. There was talk of fearful training routines, including a toughening process known as the "Hamburger Drill." A jury found in favor of Kush, who was promptly hired by the Hamilton Tiger-Cats of the Canadian Football League. Irsay, perhaps proving once and for all how out of touch he was with the psychology of the modern football player, brought him to Baltimore for the 1982 season.

The Colts were even more wretched than before. Elway's claim that the climate of Baltimore was the problem was treated lightly by most observers, correctly as it turned out. Denver Broncos negotiated away Baltimore's rights to Elway in June, just weeks after their city's airport had been closed by a blizzard.

JOHNNY UNITAS: A DIAMOND FOUND IN A SANDLOT

Watching the entire Elway performance, the dickering, the statements of the agents, the talk-show appearances was a mild-mannered, middle-aged Baltimore restaurateur and sometime television sports commentator named Johnny Unitas. Unitas was invited to one of the television shows. His most eloquent comment was his facial expression. It was an expression that spoke not so much of outrage as incomprehension and disbelief. Eventually he admitted, "I just don't know what's going on these days. I guess the world has changed."

Unitas was frankly befuddled by the notion of a college football player turning his nose up at a major American city and a famous football club. He said quietly, "The thing is, John Elway hasn't thrown the football in a professional game yet. We don't really know if he can do it."

Those who knew Unitas best felt that beneath the air of puzzlement was something deeper, something to do with changing values, changing attitudes. They sensed a little anger, a little regret at the way the game and the world had gone. Johnny Unitas had come into football with none of the fanfare of John Elway. But he stayed for eighteen years, and they were mostly superb years, persuading many that no one had ever played quarterback as well as Johnny Unitas.

He always insisted that playing quarterback was like working on the engine of a car. It was pretty straightforward once you understood where all the parts went. For Unitas quarterbacking was a job he knew he could do well and he was ready to accept all of it—the bone-jarring collisions with frozen ground, the constant requirement to deliver the big play, the game-breaking move, the sense that if he failed, so too did the team. He reveled in that responsibility. To him it was a sober mission. He did not see himself as a star. He was a technician, a man who put together a performance, under fire certainly but without histrionics. Other people could have the glory, and he had no longing for the Californian sunshine. He would accept simply the year-by-year satisfaction of turning in a technically flawless effort. By the end of his career he had compiled a formidable list of injuries, including a punctured lung, but there had never been the hint of a whine. When Elway said he did not like the thought of throwing the football in the cold of Baltimore, it was almost as though one of the greatest careers in the history of the game had been dismissed. If Baltimore was warm enough for Johnny Unitas, many felt it should be warm enough for anyone, including the hotshot kid from California.

For a while it seemed that the NFL would have no use for Unitas. He played semi-pro ball in Pittsburgh, scrambling in sandlots, refining his game, daydreaming, some said. In 1956 the Baltimore Colts rescued him from this obscurity. It was the making of the club. In 1958 Unitas gave a classic performance in a game that many insisted was the greatest in the history of professional football. The Colts beat the New York Giants in the NFL title game in Yankee Stadium. Unitas fashioned every yard of the Baltimore triumph. With just ninety seconds left, the Colts trailed by 3 points. They had possession of the ball but on their own 14-yard line. Unitas had to manipulate the clock—which is stopped at the completion of each play—and also to eat up the ground. He did so with a wonderfully fluent arm. Four passes swept the Colts to the Giants' 20-yard line, where Baltimore signalled for the field goal kicker. Steve Myhra fired the ball between the posts for the equalizing points. In extra time Unitas showed exactly what it was to be on top of the game. He moved the Colts 80 yards, briskly, with absolute authority, delivering the touchdown almost as a formality. After the game he was questioned about his decision to throw a pass on a second down 8 yards from the line. Was he not frightened by the prospect of an interception?

Unitas was appalled by the question. He said that when he made a call he assumed that it would succeed. Without such confidence, Unitas suggested, a quarterback was nothing. A quarterback had to believe in himself. If he didn't, his team had no foundation. It would be blown in the wind.

When he left football in the early 1970s—having made the mistake of moving to San Diego for one last year, a year that he recognized quickly enough would do nothing for his reputation or his sense of achievement—his own rigid value system had been overtaken by a man who lacked many of his qualities but symbolized the good life.

NAMATH: A GENIUS FOR GETTING CLOSE TO THE MARK

The quarterback who climbed above Johnny Unitas in the imagination of the American people was flippant where Unitas was profound, self-indulgent where Unitas was austere, a shameless self-promoter where Unitas sought to unify the team. But he had a quality that soared beyond virtue, beyond even the ability to win football games consistently. Namath had something that had been thin on the football ground: charm and, American advertisers realized quickly enough, sex appeal of an extremely high octane. Millions of American men wanted not to be the father of Joe Namath, as later they might think of John Elway. They wanted to *be* Joe Namath. They wanted the life of the man who was christened Broadway Joe when he joined the New York Jets from the University of Alabama in 1964.

Namath grew up in Pennsylvania, the son of Hungarian immigrants. He was by no means the classic quarterback. He was swarthy, with long, dark hair and a broad, impudent smile. What he had was presence and a willingness to step outside the traditional expectations of a football man. Namath wanted everything the game could offer. He wanted to be a Manhattan celebrity. He opened a bar, which quickly became a place at which to be seen. His comments to sports writers were outrageous. When asked to explain a humilating defeat, he snapped, "I guess it was the booze and the broads." It was said that he left a bottle of Johnny Walker Black Label and a blonde in his room before he went to play in the 1969 Super Bowl in Miami's Orange Bowl. If it was true, there was no question of club discipline. Namath made himself for life in the Orange Bowl that day.

It was a superb performance for two reasons. It showed a wonderful appreciation of the dynamics of football, of the way to dominate a game systematically. And—vital to Namath's image—it was clear that he did much of his own thinking. He tinkered with the game plan, used initiative in situations where a less self-assured quarterback might have fallen back on the announcements from the sideline. Going into the game, the Baltimore Colts were rated 21-point favorites. It was a gambler's prediction that was humiliating to Namath and the Jets. Three touchdowns is a huge margin by which to tip a big game. It was a gesture of contempt toward the old American Football League, which had recently merged with the NFL. The Jets were upstarts from an inferior league. The Colts were established power. Namath might delight the New York newspapers with his quips, his irreverent view of the old game, but he would get his comeuppance in the Florida sunshine. Unitas was out, injured, but his replacement, Earl Morrall, had won the respect of the fans and the critics. Morrall would be sound; Namath would be flashy. Soundness would win, according to the prophets.

Namath was asked about the 21-point prediction, the suggestion that there would be no serious contest. "Baloney," he declared. "We'll beat the Colts. I guarantee it." Namath's guarantee was never threatened. It was Morrall who cracked under the pressure. He threw three interceptions. Namath, droll, almost extravagantly casual, set up the running game with the hard-driving Matt Snell, then, with the offensive team nicely settled, began to probe and tease the Colts' cover with a series of completed passes to another free-spirited, long-haired character, wide receiver George Sauer. Namath sent in Snell for the New York touchdown and controlled the play sufficiently for Jim Turner to kick three field goals. Morrall could never approach such control, and in the last quarter the Colts sent in the wounded Unitas. The great man simply had too much to do. He engineered a downfield drive that ended with a 1-yard touchdown from running back Jerry Hill. The Jets won by 16 points to 7. Namath saluted the vast crowd, imperiously, a young general hungry for the fruits of victory. He raised his right arm to the darkening sky and stuck out his index finger. The Jets, New York, Joe Namath were number one. The great monster of a city and much of the United States would always love him for his afternoon's work.

I first met Namath in a dark and somewhat musty television studio in a rundown neighborhood on the west side of New York. Namath was making a commercial for pantyhose. Off-camera he was a little dry, and there was a hint of self-mockery. It was early in 1976, and Namath's football career had run down from the glory of Miami seven years earlier. Plagued by knee injuries, he had known many moments of brilliance on the field, but his career after Super Bowl III had been something of an anti-climax. The image he had presented that January afternoon had grown beyond the sum of his talent.

He smiled a little sadly and reported that recently he had played an informal game on Rikers Island, New York, which had been watched by convicts. "I threw a bad pass," said Namath, "and one of the guys from the prison shouted, 'If you throw any more passes like that, Broadway Joe, you're gonna be Bowery Joe pretty damned quick.' I had to laugh. Ever since I started in pro football I've realized that one bad hit or a few bad games can make you history. So, yes, I guess I did work on the image. I did try to give myself some professional life outside the game.

"Now I'm taking acting lessons and I've got some movie parts. When the knees really hurt and when I think the football might be over, it's comforting to know there are other things for me. I'm grateful to football for that. I guess it gave me a stage I never would have had otherwise. But I don't get too sentimental. I think I made a contribution too. Maybe I brought a bit of humor to it."

New York's love affair with Joe Namath would linger, but as we talked it was clear that he realized that the old intensity had vanished. Nowhere on this earth demands professional perform-ance as insistently as New York City, and the truth was that Namath's value as a quarterback was about over. A few weeks later he would be traded to the Los Angeles Rams; forlornly, he would string out a career which had been colored by every shade but gray.

As we talked, Namath from time to time fired a wad of chewing tobacco from his mouth to a tin can a few feet across his dingy dressing-room. After five hits I remarked that there was little wrong with his accuracy. "I guess I've been lucky," he said. "Whatever I've tried to do, I've generally been close to the mark."

In terms of his acting career this claim was to prove less than prophetic. He performed somewhat leadenly in his Hollywood exposures, but then his name remained magnetic and his charm did not go the way of his knees. His devoted New York agent, Jimmy Walsh, was always able to conjure work, a stage show here, a nightclub performance there. And Broadway Joe always drew them in. For most Americans football had become more than a game; it was a statement about the pressures and the opportunities of life, and no one had taken his chance more cleanly than Namath.

Football critics, especially those who consider themselves purists, guardians of the game's best qualities, have tended to be hard on Namath. There is a suggestion that he abused his gifts, that in a man of more sobriety his talent would have reached dazzling levels. It is certainly true that persistent injuries deprived Namath of much in his prime, and it may be true that he never put together a sufficient body of work for him to be judged alongside the greatest of all quarterbacks. But this is perhaps a narrow view. No one could question the range of Namath's skills in 1972, when he tore apart the vaunted defense of the Colts, throwing for six touchdowns and 496 yards. In that same season he put Oakland Raiders to the sword, and members of the Californian team shook their heads and talked darkly of sorcery.

Perhaps the soundest conclusion is that Joe Namath's appetite for football was overtaken by his appetite for life and that, happily, he did not have to pay the price exacted from many less gifted athletes and less charming human beings. In *The Pro Football A to Z* there is a quotation from a teammate of Namath that helps to explain his hold on the American people. Wide receiver Jerome Barkum turned to Namath in the middle of a mesmerizing performance and said, "You're the hottest thing since fire."

In Unitas there was ice and in Namath there was fire. It is possible so to categorize quarterbacks because no position on the football field demands such unequivocal statements of personality. Through all of them, though, there is a unifying thread. Quarterbacks have to believe in themselves, and they have to possess the kind of courage that is implicit. Nothing so destroys the morale of a team as a hint that the quarterback's nerve may be in question.

There also has to be very deep-rooted self-confidence. It is extraordinary to examine the backgrounds of the game's current leading quarterbacks. Almost without exception, they tell a story of adversity, of physical injury and some psychological scarring. Namath's successor in the Jets, Richard Todd, has had to undergo seven years of fighting to replace a legend. In 1982 it seemed that Todd had at last begun to assign Namath to the pages of history. On a freezing December afternoon Todd, a blond Southerner, deftly picked his way through the defense of the Buffalo Bills and led the Jets to the American Football Conference final against Miami Dolphins. The New York fans, some of them bare-chested in their exuberance, chanted Todd's name in Shea Stadium. But it was a different story in the Florida sunshine. Todd was put under fierce pressure by the Miami defense, and at a critical moment he threw into the arms of Miami linebacker A. J. Duhe, who promptly galloped over the New York line.

For Todd the implications of that interception were horrendous. It meant that he had returned to the very starting line of his professional career, to that time when he followed Namath from the University of Alabama to New York in the mid-1970s. Had he driven the Jets to victory over Miami, he would have inched closer to the quarterback's ideal of being number one, unchallenged in the confidence of the coach and the public. As it happened, in the hearts of New York's aggressive fans he would remain Richard Who?, and he would continue to be vulnerable to the drafting of a talented young replacement or a move by the club into the market for an experienced, "money" player. Of course, all of professional sport is redolent with such insecurity, but in American football the sense of it is heightened by the exposure of college football. A player in Todd's precarious position can watch some young Turk bidding for his job on national television.

THE FEARS AND THE FEUDS

Some manifestations of this pressure can be truly ugly. One of the worst cases occurred over the last few years in Los Angeles, where Pat Haden and Vince Ferragamo found themselves disputing the Rams' quarterback position. Haden and Ferragamo were sharply contrasting figures. Haden was blond, a mere 5 feet 11 inches, and he brought with him a brilliant academic record from the University of Southern California, where he qualified as a Rhodes Scholar. Ferragamo was taller, dark and pure athlete. Physically he was, according to one writer, "a high school girl's dream."

It was little surprise that the fans sided with Ferragamo. Much of professional football is to do with fantasy, and he was custom-made for the part. His right arm was much stronger than Haden's. Ferragamo threw bombs. Haden nagged and flicked at the opposition. And then there was a movie made by Warren Beatty, entitled *Heaven Can Wait*, that concerned a young football player restored to life and a starring role with the Los Angeles Rams. He happened to be a quarterback. Ferragamo remarked, "I guess I do look a little like Warren Beatty."

Late in 1979 it seemed that Ferragamo had turned Beatty's role into reality. Midway through the season Haden was injured. When it was announced over the public address system of the Los Angeles Coliseum that Haden's injury was serious, that he would not return to the game, there were thunderous cheers. Haden the quarterback died a little that afternoon: "You hear those cheers when you feel your career has been wrecked, and I guess it's inevitable that you have bitter feelings. Quarterbacks are only human." Briefly, Ferragamo appeared superhuman. He led the Rams to a Super Bowl appearance, and he did it with soaring confidence, shaping the upset of the season with the defeat of Dallas Cowboys in their bastion of Texas Stadium.

On a glorious afternoon in Pasadena in January Ferragamo brushed against the splendor Namath had found in Miami more than a decade earlier. He was confronted by the Pittsburgh Steelers in the XIVth Super Bowl. The Steelers had dominated the League in recent years under their cool, methodical coach Chuck Noll. They had awesome strength in both offense and defense. No one threw the long ball better than quarterback Bradshaw, and there was a superb corps of receivers headed by the graceful Swann and the explosive John Stallworth. Along the ground Harris ran with flair, and he received dogged support from Vietnam veteran Rocky Blier. The offensive line was led brilliantly by Mike Webster, generally considered the best center in football. In defense the Steelers had the volcanic presence of Mean Joe Greene at defensive tackle, and behind there was the brains and sinew of middle linebacker Jack Lambert and the hitting power of Robin Cole. Heaven may have been waiting for Ferragamo, but there was a suspicion in Pasadena that he might catch a little hell.

Ferragamo caught hell, certainly, but not until the sun began to sink beyond the mountains that ring the Rose Bowl. Before the dusk Ferragamo had moments even more spectacular than those of Namath in Miami. Four times Ferragamo cocked his right arm and threw for touchdowns. The impassive Noll began to wince at the ease with which Ferragamo found holes in his cover. But, unlike Namath, Ferragamo could not hold his team together. The immense strength of the Steelers began to drain the Rams of their resolve; Ferragamo's protection began to dwindle, and in the fourth quarter he threw an interception. The veteran Bradshaw, steadying himself after some erratic work, decided it was time to go home. He hit Stallworth with two long passes. Ferragamo had been close, but in those last minutes the door was slammed.

There was no Hollywood ending. When Haden completed his rehabilitation, the Los Angeles coach, Ray Malavasi, announced that he would return as number one. Ferragamo had to revert to his old role of challenger. The situation had been clouded by rancorous contract negotiations between Ferragamo and the club. Ferragamo's agent complained that the player was vague, difficult and perhaps under the influence of his wife Jody, the daughter of a wrestler.

Into the impasse came a free-wheeling overnight multimillionaire from Canada. Nelson Skalbania had made his money in Vancouver real estate, and almost before he had turned his first million he was dabbling in the dream world of professional sport. He bought an ice hockey club in Indianapolis and signed the *Wunderkind* of the game, a tousled-headed teenager from Ontario named Wayne Gretzky. He also bought a soccer club in Atlanta and a half-share in a Vancouver baseball club bidding for major league status. Inevitably, Skalbania's tentacles reached into football. He took over the Canadian Football League (CFL) club Montreal Alouettes and had visions of filling more than 70,000 seats at the Olympic Stadium. Skalbania concluded that Ferragamo, the Hollywood quarterback, would fill his stadium. He offered the player nearly $1 million dollars for a two-year contract. Ferragamo was reluctant to leave Los Angeles, but here was financial security for life. Admittedly, there were a few snags. Ferragamo would have at least to make gestures toward learning French, a prerequisite for mass popularity in the violently francophone city. He would also have to make adjustments to his play. The Canadian field was bigger and there were twelve players rather than eleven.

"Sure, I'll have to make some changes," said Ferragamo, "but I just couldn't say no to Mr. Skalbania's offer. It's a very generous one, and at 27 years of age I can think in terms of a good career in Canada and maybe another one back in the NFL."

Canadian football fans were thrilled. The CFL draws fervent support from the prairie towns of Regina and Winnipeg, Calgary and Edmonton, but in the big cities of Toronto, Vancouver and Montreal there is a sense that it is overshadowed wholly by the NFL, whose games are available live on American television networks beaming into Canada. The CFL club is staffed by a statutory number (fifteen) of Americans who have been either shunned or missed by the NFL's elaborate scouting system. Ferragamo was a prize, a jewel. He was a Super Bowl quarterback. Here was real glamour, a real-life hero from the city of dreams. Skalbania preened himself, announced that other Canadian club owners should pay him for his gift to the League. Ferragamo would fill stadiums from Montreal, Toronto, Hamilton and Ottawa in the east all the way to Vancouver on the Pacific.

It was a nice dream, but it didn't last through one game. Writers and television crews from all over the United States descended on Vancouver's Empire Stadium—where Sir Roger Bannister and John Landy ran their Miracle Mile—to witness the debut of the quarterback in exile. Ferragamo was shaky and uncertain, and it was clear that he had not yet adjusted to the new dimensions of the Canadian field and the fact that four downs had been replaced by three. As the British Columbia Lions annihilated his Alouettes, Skalbania held his breath and said that it was a time for patience.

Skalbania's patience—and his resources—failed quickly enough. Ferragamo never adjusted to Canadian football. His dream did not travel well from southern California, and around the time when Nelson Skalbania was making arrangements with his creditors, who were owed something in the region of $30 million, Ferragamo was reporting contritely for duty with the Los Angeles Rams again.

Like Todd in New York and at least a dozen other quarterbacks across the country, Ferragamo had to rebuild. The old bombs had faded from memory. What mattered was how he performed today. Could he ever again read NFL defenses as well as he did in those dramatic days in the winter of 1979–80? Had the Canadian experience wrecked his belief in himself? The jury remains out on Vince Ferragamo, and heaven is proving a little more elusive than it seemed when he moved to within an inch of glory under the nose of Mean Joe Greene.

But then every quarterback has known this pressure. Bob Waterfield, the Los Angeles Ram whose bold throwing in the late 1940s and early 1950s introduced the word "bomb" into football, suffered the pressure of a Pat Haden when the brilliant young Norm Van Brocklin emerged as a challenger. For several seasons these great players dueled for the number one status, and Waterfield learned that his old triumphs meant little against the promise of a dazzling newcomer.

Van Brocklin was christened the Flying Dutchman. His basic technique was quite simple. He stepped into the pocket, the area of protection created by center, guards and tackles, and waited impassively for possibilities to present themselves downfield. It was nerveless football, profoundly thrilling to the fans. Van Brocklin, who died suddenly in 1982, had many imitators. Among modern players the closest adherents to his style are probably Dan Fouts of San Diego and Pittsburgh's Bradshaw.

If he had had to choose a year, Van Brocklin would have picked 1951. He led the Rams to the NFL title, and at New York's Polo Grounds he destroyed the Yanks—a franchise that survived just two years in the NFL—with passing that seemed to operate on some private radar system. He threw for a record 554 yards. In the NFL final he produced a superb *coup de grâce*, a 73-yard touchdown pass.

Soon enough Van Brocklin experienced the kind of threat he had earlier offered to Waterfield. After several years of uncertainty, he lost his place to a new favorite of the crowd, Billy Wade. But if Van Brocklin's arm was made in heaven, his will was forged in a less tranquil place. He moved to Philadelphia and led the Eagles to an Eastern Conference title. It was an improbable triumph for a man who was considered past his best, and it contained an extraordinary statistic. Eight times the Philadelphia Eagles went trailing into the last quarter. Eight times Van Brocklin lifted them for a winning effort.

The Flying Dutchman found less fulfillment as coach of the Minnesota Vikings in Minneapolis and was immediately embroiled in controversy with reigning quarterback Fran Tarkenton. Tarkenton's rambling, scrambling style of quarterbacking deeply offended Van Brocklin. He had always played in the pocket, using an invisible howitzer to pound opposing defenses, and Tarkenton's act was an affront to his sense of how the game would be played. The relationship between coach and quarterback is vital to any club; if it is unsatisfactory, the team is without a rudder. Eventually, Tarkenton refused to play under Van Brocklin, who then handed in his own resignation.

Van Brocklin surfaced briefly in 1968 as coach of the Atlanta Falcons, but his inability to communicate productively with his players led to his early dismissal. He had been a great, brave player, but he couldn't translate his skills and courage into coaching. It is a familiar story in many professional sports, but there was perhaps a special poignancy to Van Brocklin's position. On the field he had been masterful, in control of events. Off the field it was as though he was left just the old love of combat, of standing in the middle of the battle, shaping the conflict to his own design. After the Atlanta Falcons had been soundly beaten in one game, a writer asked him if he was still a fighter. The Flying Dutchman said that indeed he was. He would prove it to the questioner; he would prove it to the whole damned press conference. Writers, photographers and broadcasters were all invited to put up their fists. It was a rather tragic scene. It was another glimpse into the dark side of the glory game.

For Van Brocklin the tragedy was that he could not let go. He could have made a comfortable living outside the game or in one of its many soft areas of promotion, local broadcasting or public relations. There are many such sinecures for the great ones. But he could not leave the sideline, the pit of conflict. He could not forget that once he had been a great American quarterback, arguably the greatest of all time.

THE QUARTERBACK: MAN OF DESTINY

There is no shortage of contenders for such a title. Bobby Layne might have claimed it in the 1950s had he not been so easily diverted into saloons and nightclubs. He operated for fifteen years, enjoying his best days in Detroit, where he led the Lions to two NFL championships. He was tough and bright and, unlike Van Brocklin, he sensed that the game had changed and that maybe there was no longer a place for him at its competitive heart. He returned to his native Lubbock, Texas, set himself up in business and said later, wistfully, "We were a lot closer as a group when I played. We used to do things together, the whole team. It's not like that now."

Slingin' Sammy Baugh, another Texan, is generally accepted as the father of modern quarterbacks. He was signed by the extrovert Washington Redskins owner George Marshall in 1937. He was a wiry, taciturn character who turned the forward pass from an act of desperation into a threat. His great rival, Sid Luckman of the Chicago Bears, conceded, "No one can pass the football like Sammy Baugh."

Baugh made the first definitive statement on the way a quarterback could control a game; from being a versatile and important member of the offensive unit the quarterback became the man of destiny. One of his staunchest admirers was the great Y. A. (Yelverton Abraham) Tittle, whose seventeen-year career took him from Baltimore to San Francisco to New York. He never won an NFL title, and there were times when the frustration of it overwhelmed him. When the Giants lost the NFL title to the Bears in 1963 Tittle bowed his head and wept at the close of the game. Helped by pain-killing drugs, he had attempted to play on a badly injured left leg. But he could not achieve balance, and five of his last six throws were intercepted. He had to settle for the regard of his fellow pros and the aficionados' view that Tittle had brought many refinements to the art proclaimed by Slingin' Sam. Tittle recalled, "Kids in my part of Texas would rather play football than eat. Sammy Baugh was our idol, and we all spent hours pitching footballs through old tires hung from tree limbs, the way we had seen Baugh do it in the newsreels."

Tittle, Bart Starr, the unspectacular general of the Green Bay Packers, scrambling, fearless Roger Staubach of the Dallas Cowboys—all brought their particular gifts to the job of quarterbacking. They changed it from a job to an almost mystical calling. To see this vocation celebrated most spectacularly, today the place to go is San Diego's Jack Murphy Stadium, where Dan Fouts is the resident flamethrower. Fouts, a bearded, somewhat eccentric loner, spends the off-season months in the woods of Oregon. In the season he throws the ball more boldly, more imaginatively, than any of his contemporaries. For five years now the Chargers have been football's most

spectacular team. Fouts has superb targets. Tight end Kellen
Winslow is considered by some to be the game's finest athlete.
He explodes from the line of scrimmage with a magnificent
hauteur, and his hands are so safe they might be covered with
adhesive. Winslow stands 6 feet 5 inches tall and weighs more
than 240 pounds. Wes Chandler and Charlie Joiner are traditional receivers, wily, quick, and masters of pace and deception.
Watching the Chargers rolling downfield is to see the full
potential of the game. They swallow the field with their speed,
their sublime confidence. The problems come when they lose the
ball, something that has to happen from time to time even to an
offensive unit as accomplished as this one. Invariably, the San
Diego defense crumbles in the big games. Fouts confers with his
coach Don Coryell on the sideline. They shake their heads and
look at the sky. San Diego need a Mean Joe Greene and a Jack
Lambert and a Hacksaw Reynolds, killer defenders. Then the
glory of Dan Fouts might be redeemed. Until that happens he
will remain in limbo—a magnificent limbo, certainly, but limbo
all the same.

Jim Plunkett stepped out of the shadows in the last months of
1980. He led the Oakland Raiders to a Super Bowl win over the
Philadelphia Eagles in the New Orleans Superdome, became a
genuine American hero but did not linger long at the after-game
celebrations in the French quarter. He slipped away into the
night, a complex, somewhat troubled young man who had
perhaps seen too much of the dark side of the pro game.

His career would probably have dwindled away without
notice had Oakland's number one Don Pastorini not suffered a
broken leg. Pastorini was a more obvious quarterback type.
Long-haired, dashing, he was briefly married to an actress and
prided himself on his physical courage and willingness to make
the big, brave plays. Irritated by the criticisms of a local reporter
during his service with the Houston Oilers, Pastorini took the
writer to one side and knocked him down.

Plunkett merely smoldered as he traced the steady decline of a
career that started brilliantly at Stanford University. He was
born of poor Mexican parents in San José, 30 miles south of San
Francisco, and was always conscious that his football salary—
and his degree from Stanford—had been won against the
heaviest of odds. Plunkett was chosen first in the 1971 college
draft but, as is so often the case, the honor was dubious. He was

taken by the New England Patriots, who were then the worst team in football. The Patriots proved inept in the business of protecting their star quarterback. He had two knee and three shoulder operations in five years and was traded to the San Francisco 49ers. The 49ers play at Candlestick Park, a draughty stadium perched on a promontory of San Francisco Bay. For Plunkett Candlestick Park was the coldest place on earth.

He told *Sports Illustrated* writer Rick Telander, "I really thought I was going to be the savior, but all I did was put more pressure on myself. San Francisco was by far the worst experience of my life. It felt like the whole world was falling in on me." San Francisco's coach Joe Thomas became the one man in professional football Plunkett admits to actively disliking. "He's the kind of guy who prides himself on being the man who got rid of Johnny Unitas instead of respecting what Unitas did for the game. I'm sorry, but I'm not big enough not to have a grudge against him."

Plunkett drifted to the Raiders, where it seemed as though he would languish behind the erratic but glamorous Pastorini. Yet he made it in the end. He came through in the way that quarterbacks are expected to come through, rather as John Wayne, a quarterback in his own college days, came through in *True Grit*. Plunkett coolly plotted victory in the Superdome, but it was as though he had known too much disappointment. He could not celebrate his victory. He told an interviewer on a breakfast television show, "Nothing recedes like success." He also said, "A cliché I use frequently is the one about going from the penthouse to the outhouse in a short time.

"I think I understand sports better now than before. It's a business. All the hero worship does the athletes some good—we get money and endorsements—but it does the fans a whole lot of good. They live through us. I think I'm a fairly good human being. I try to be honest and fair. But I've done some things I'm not too proud of, things I don't have any explanation for. And I think I've been painted as too good a guy overall.

"During my first year in New England I thought, 'Hey, there's nothing to this. I'm going to have a fun time in the NFL.' Then in 1972 my confidence ran into a stone wall. I'd never been in a losing situation before, not even in high school, and the more I worked the worse things got. If I played bad, we lost; if I played good, we still lost. I took everything too hard on myself. I tried to throw for a touchdown on every play, to make everything up at once. But now I try not to worry about things I don't have control over."

What Plunkett has perhaps grasped is the essential challenge of playing quarterback. Whatever you do, there is no way of avoiding the inevitable. One day you will hear the boos of the crowd. They came to Van Brocklin and to Tittle and even to the beloved Namath; they are part of the cycle of quarterbacking. The quarterback *is* the team. He rides its glory and is punished most heavily for its defeats.

There are different ways of dealing with such inevitability. You can be Joe Montana of the 49ers, the Super Bowl hero of 1982. You can buy Arab thoroughbreds and get a tough agent to negotiate a good contract that will insulate you against the worst of the pain. You can be like Kenny Stabler, a veteran of the League who is bidding once more for the big triumphs, this time with the New Orleans Saints. They call Stabler the "Snake." He has guts and flair and great swaggering panache in the final stages of a game. He followed Joe Namath from the University of Alabama and, like Broadway Joe, realized that the most expensive quarterbacks tend to develop a colorful off-field persona. Stabler has been warned about gambling companions, about his imperious attitude to club discipline. But he has never been rejected by the League because he has presence, the promise of the right stuff.

Some thought Archie Manning might be the quarterback of the late 1970s. He was strong and resilient and had a magnificent right arm. But he too was obliterated by the draft. He joined the New Orleans Saints, who were as feeble in the protection of their quarterback as they were in most other aspects of the game. In 1980, the year that New Orleans fans took to wearing paper bags over their heads, Manning touched despair.

In November of that year I spoke with him in his stall in the Superdome dressing-room. New Orleans had been overpowered by the Los Angeles Rams. When Manning took off his padding you could see the damage of the season in bruises and welts and taping. But it was his eyes that you noticed most. They seemed to be unseeing.

Eventually he said, "You come into the pros with so much hope, so much expectation, because you've got used to the feeling of winning. You think it will always be like that. But then when the winning stops, I tell you, it's the worst trip. This season there have been times when I've wanted to run away from New Orleans. You get tired of going out and hearing the remarks, the bad remarks. And it touches every part of your life. And then you think that if you ran away, it would be with you for the rest of your life. So you go on, take the hits, even though you know it's hopeless. I guess the trick is to realize that you're only as good as the team, you can only try to do the best you can."

In the summer of 1983 Manning was with the Houston Oilers, weighing his chances against those of a younger man. Then, suddenly, he was traded to the Minnesota Vikings. He had been a professional quarterback for thirteen years. He had no inclination to call young John Elway and say that he was wrong to hold the NFL to ransom. He knew better than most that if you have a bargaining position it is wise to use it before a mad-dog linebacker catches you on the blindside or a huge lineman rearranges your ribcage. He knew that when football offers a flash of glory, it also guarantees pain. For a quarterback the glory sometimes lasts no longer than the throwing of an interception. Often the pain is for life.

6

The Black Division

Ollie Matson could do almost anything on a football field. He ran beautifully. He was elusive enough to play halfback. He had the genuine power required of a fullback. Send him in as a wide receiver and he would run for you a wonderful pattern. His hands were safe too. He saw only the ball, none of the physical hazards that tend to tug at the attention of those less than totally committed, the elbow in the kidneys, the fist in the gut. Defensive backs generally went down like skittles when they attempted to intervene.

If you were stuck for a tight end, Matson could fill in very nicely. He threw a heavy block, found space in the most congested traffic, and again there were the good hands for the bullet pass, which needs to be cradled against the impact of heavy collision. Trouble in the defensive secondary? Send in Matson. He could pick up the offensive play in a moment, adjust and cover the ground. An offense would have to think twice about burning Ollie Matson with a long bomb.

Chicago Cardinals snapped him up when he graduated from the University of San Francisco. In 1959 Los Angeles Rams' general manager, Pete Rozelle, who is now the commissioner of the NFL, was so impressed with Matson that he offered nine players in exchange for his services. The Cardinals, a little bemused, accepted the trade. Detroit Lions signed him in 1963, and a year later the Philadelphia Eagles saw him as the man to solve several of their problems. He retired with much honor in 1966. For fourteen years he had been a superb professional.

Only two positions were truly beyond Matson. He could not play on the line because he was not big enough, and he could not play quarterback because he was black.

SCALING A "JAGGED OUTCROP OF TRUTH"

Bizarre as it may seem so many years after Little Rock and Martin Luther King, the truth is that only one NFL club has recently had the courage to invest in the development of a black quarterback. The club is Tampa Bay, and the quarterback is Doug Williams, a graduate of the predominantly black Grambling College in Louisiana. Ironically, Williams decided to jump to the USFL in the fall of 1983. What the NFL is saying, when you cut through a blanket of hypocrisy, is that the black athlete can do wonderful things for your football team—he can run like Campbell and Dorsett, Simpson and Brown, catch like Stallworth and Swann, rampage like Mean Joe Greene—but he cannot lead. He cannot hand out instructions to white teammates. There are two other positions where the percentage of black players drops dramatically. One is middle linebacker, the defensive counterpoint to the quarterback. The other is center, captain of the offensive line. These places are reserved almost exclusively for whites. The quarterback has to reach down to take the ball from between the center's legs. The middle linebacker is a figure of authority.

Over the past thirty years fewer than two dozen black quarterbacks have been granted any kind of chance in the NFL, and of these only Tampa's Williams established himself in the job. Ever since baseball's Brooklyn Dodgers allowed the great Jackie Robinson to break the color line in 1946, the black athlete has appeared to make tremendous strides. He dominates the lucrative world of basketball and has secured some of baseball's largest salaries. Moses Malone recently signed a $13.2 million contract with basketball's Philadelphia 76ers. New York Yankees awarded Dave Winfield a $12 million deal, a generous enough admission that few people had ever hit the baseball so hard, caught it so cleanly and thrown it with such phenomenal strength. Sugar Ray Leonard, welterweight champion of the world before his retirement in 1982, earned more than $30 million, the richest haul in the history of professional sports. When Kareem Abdul Jabbar's Los Angeles home burned down early in 1983, the insurance claim told a story of staggering wealth—of exquisite Persian carpets, of fine art. But still only Doug Williams received a sustained opportunity to call the plays in NFL football.

Mention this exclusion of blacks from professional football's most influential position to the average coach or NFL official, and the odds are you will get an elaborate explanation. It will studiously avoid even a hint of racism. There will be two strands to the explanation. They can be placed under the sub-headings "Great Athlete syndrome" and "Wrong background." The first theory claims that black quarterbacks are often such great athletes that they can be employed immediately at another position, usually wide receiver or defensive back, rather than languishing on the bench while acquiring the "background knowledge" considered essential for quarterbacks graduating to the professional game. The second suggests that black quarterbacks suffer in their early training and begin their pro careers at a disadvantage.

This second theory can be broken down into two premises. The first is that a black quarterback has trained at a college that does not offer first-rate coaching. The second is that the athlete has attended a school that does not employ a "pro system" of offense, which is to say, one based on the passing game. Before 1970 there was perhaps some validity to the first premise. Many black athletes, especially those from the southern United States, attended segregated schools. These schools were often shortchanged in their government funding, and their athletic programs were shoe-string affairs when compared to the big white colleges, notably the Crimson Tide of Alabama and the Bulldogs of Georgia.

This argument is fine as far as it goes and superficially shifts some of the responsibility for the absence of professional black quarterbacks from the NFL to old social ills and in-built racism in the South. But it has a major flaw, which lies in the fact that many of the current NFL quarterbacks have emerged from small colleges. Ken Anderson, who led the Cincinnati Bengals to the 1982 Super Bowl, learned to quarterback at the small Augustana College, Illinois. The famous Bradshaw threw the ball for lightweight Louisiana Tech. St Louis Cardinals got both their quarterbacks from small colleges, Neil Lomax from Portland State and Jim Hart from Southern Illinois. Philadelphia's Ron Jaworksi, one of the League's more respected quarterbacks, graduated from obscure Youngstown State, Ohio, and the eternally promising Jim Zorn of Seattle popped up from California Polytechnic-Pomona.

To underline further the emptiness of the "poor background" argument is the fact that over the last ten years several black quarterbacks have performed brilliantly for powerful schools. Condredge Holloway, a small but marvelously brave quarterback, led Tennessee to three play-off bowl games; Homer Jordan guided Clemson to number one ranking in the nation; and Warren Moon carried the University of Washington to the prestigious Rose Bowl title.

Not one of these three excellent players created a flicker of interest in the NFL. All three of them headed for Canada, prompting the dry, sad observation that they were following the old trail of escaping slaves. Moon and Holloway have been particularly successful in Canada.

Holloway remains the key factor in the "run-and-shoot" offense of the Toronto Argonauts, a system that involves "extra motion" at the line of scrimmage and a quarterback who can scramble bravely. It is a system built on the quick wits of the quarterback, on his instinctive feel for offensive possibilities. In one important game in the 1983 season Holloway was shorn of protection from his offensive line and was hit by a defensive end and a linebacker. The hits were simultaneous and from two directions. The ebullient Holloway raised himself smartly to his feet and strode off the field almost jauntily. He was not retreating, Toronto having to punt the ball after three downs. When Holloway reached the sideline and the cover of his own team, he fell to the ground, groaning. Within minutes he was back on the field, directing a winning effort. Later he xplained, "When somebody nearly kills you on the football field, the last thing you want to show is that you felt it." It was revealed later that Holloway had sustained two cracked ribs.

Moon led Edmonton Eskimos to three Grey Cup triumphs with his tremendous right arm and his absolute refusal to panic. At one point he agreed to sign a series of ten one-year contracts with the Canadian club. It was a sign of his grim acceptance that the color line would deny him his chance of making it in the big league south of the border. Then, in 1982, the new USFL was announced, and Moon changed his mind about the chance of a journey home. He said that he had achieved all he could in Canada. Gnawing at him was his belief that he could play quarterback in the NFL as well as any of the blond superstars who each weekend decorated network television.

More than half the number one quarterbacks in the Canadian Football League are now black. It is a rare bonanza for the junior league. It cannot compete in salaries, but it can offer the black quarterback the chance to fulfill his own destiny.

Roy Dewalt, quarterback of the British Columbia Lions, is a

superb athlete. At his Texas college he quarterbacked a success-ful, run-orientated offense. NFL clubs were impressed with his ability to take the ball and scramble for ground. No matter that he could thread a powerful pass through a thicket of opponents. No matter that he had excellent temperament. They could see that he was big, strong and black . . . and that he could run. He was drafted by the Cleveland Browns as a running back.

Dewalt says, "Cleveland offered me a good contract, and the money was a little tempting. But then I thought about it and I said, 'Hell, no, I'm a quarterback. That's my job.' I went to Canada because those people were saying, 'We like what you can do on the field. We think you're a good quarterback.' I never really found out what Cleveland thought about me as a quarterback. My ambition now? Well, I want to prove myself more than a good quarterback, I want to prove myself a great quarterback. Maybe one day things will be different. Maybe one day an NFL club will come to me and say, 'Hey, we want you to play quarterback.' That would be neat. It would be good going home on my own terms."

Professor Harry Edwards, a radical black educator at Berkeley, argues that the refusal to accept the black quarter-back is really no more than a jagged outcrop of truth in the elaborate hoax that in sports at least his people have been granted true emancipation.

Professor Edwards writes: "For decades, student athletes, usually 17-to-19-year-old freshmen, have informally agreed to a contract with the universities they attend: athletic performance in exchange for an education. The athletes have kept their part of the bargain. The universities have not. Universities and athletic departments have gained huge gate receipts, television revenues, national visibility, donors to university programs and more as a result of the performances of gifted basketball and football players, of whom a disproportionate number of the most gifted and most exploited have been black.

"While blacks are not the only student athletes exploited, the abuses usually happen to them first and worst. To understand why, we must understand sport's impact upon black society: how popular beliefs that blacks are innately superior athletes, and that sports are 'inherently' beneficial, combine with the life circumstances of young blacks, and with the aspirations of black student athletes, to make these students especially vulnerable to victimization.

"Sports at all levels are widely believed to have achieved extraordinary, if not exemplary, advances in the realm of interracial relations since the time when Jackie Robinson became the first black to play major-league baseball. To some extent, this reputation has been deliberately fostered by skilled sports propagandists eager to project 'patriotic' views consistent with America's professed ideals of racial justice and equality of opportunity. To a much greater extent, however, this view of sports has been encouraged by observers of the sporting scene who have simply been naïve about the dynamics of sport as an institution, about their relationship to society generally, and about the race-related realities of American sports in particular."

THE BLACK RUNS, THE WHITE THROWS

Many misconceptions about race and sports can be traced to developments in sports that would appear, on the surface, to represent significant racial progress. For instance, though blacks constitute only 11.7 per cent of the US population, in 1982 more than 55 per cent of the players in the NFL were black, and in 1981 twenty-four of the twenty-eight first-round NFL draft choices were black.

"Black representation on sports honor rolls has been even more disproportionate. For example, the past nine Heisman trophies awarded each year to the best collegiate football player in the land have gone to blacks. In the final rushing statistics of the 1982 NFL season thirty-six of the top forty running backs were black. . . ." Professor Edwards is saying that the black runs with the ball; the white throws it. He is also saying, with overwhelming supporting evidence, that fellow blacks are wrong to oppose moves to toughen up academic requirements for student athletes. Edwards argues that tougher scholastic demands will mean that universities, desperate for black athletic talent, will be forced to make real efforts to provide a genuine education rather than a system devised to keep the athlete on campus as long as he is valuable to the team.

It is a vicious system. The best of the student athletes are drawn into the professional game. Those who fail to meet that standard or who are cut down by injuries that can leave them crippled are abandoned with a meaningless piece of paper and no preparation for life beyond the razzle-dazzle of the football stadium. In some of the least scrupulous of the colleges degree credits are given for basket-weaving. Annually, such abuses are uncovered. Athletic directors are fired, but the system rolls on. No one gets round to quantifying the number of personal tragedies, the hopelessness that descends when the football caravan moves off without a young man who has been trained only to hit and run with the ball. In the nationwide telecasts of college games are inserted paid messages from big-college sport's governing body, the NCAA. Honeyed voices talk of the value of college education, the building of tomorrow, usually against a film background of misty shots of ivy-covered towers, red-brick libraries.

The professor's outrage may seem a flimsy force against the weight of such propaganda, but he is not without support. Joe Paterno, the white coach of the 1982 all-conquering Penn State University, told a San Diego convention of the NCAA, "For fifteen years we have had a race problem. We have raped a generation and a half of young black athletes. We have taken the kids and sold them on bouncing a ball and running with a football and that being able to do certain things athletically was going to be an end in itself. We cannot afford to do that to another generation."

Paterno could speak with a clean conscience. Ninety per cent of his athletes graduate from college with genuine degrees. But then it is also true that Joe Paterno's star quarterback is white. Penn State's team draws huge crowds. Pennsylvania is blue-collar country. It would prefer a white quarterback.

Ultimately, it may be that the need for victory will outweigh prejudice, that an embattled owner or coach will decide that if a quarterback can run with the power of a fullback, can throw the ball as a Masai warrior hurls a spear, the color of his skin might in the last analysis be irrelevant. Certainly, there is little question that the profit motive is established more bluntly in football than in any other professional sport.

In basketball owners outbid each other in lunatic auctions for free-agent players; in baseball a once famous pitcher, Vida Blue, walked away from the game in 1983 after failing to produce one winning performance. His annual salary was $800,000. But in football there is no such largesse. Football players are by far the worst paid of American major-league sportsmen, though this is not to say that the most gifted of them are not well paid by any standard except that of baseball, basketball, boxing and the entertainment industry. Their career expectancy is a third that of baseball players. Severe injury is the probability.

The football clubs deal from a position of vast strength. If a black quarterback is too proud to run the football, well, let him pump gas or go to Canada. There are plenty more where he came from. They come in their droves to the summer training camps, and relentlessly they are pared down to the very best. Doing the paring, exclusively, are white coaches. There has never been a black head coach or general manager of an NFL club.

It has already been said that in many ways football is a perfect reflection of American society. Not too many black Americans would disagree.

7

The Magic Dragon

E ven by the standards of a Miami courtroom the tension was high. It was generated by the man in the dock, a sad-faced black whose athleticism, implicit in broad shoulders and a still perceptible waistline, was under siege from middle age and something that from time to time sent a series of shudders through his body. It seemed that of all the people in the room he alone felt a chill. Eugene "Mercury" Morris was speaking in short, choking sentences. He was appealing for a second chance. The face of the judge was impassive.

The line of appeal was more original than most. Mercury Morris was saying that drugs had destroyed his life, but that his experience should not be wasted in prison. Why not make that experience productive? Why not allow him some degree of freedom so that he could work the streets, rescue some of those kids who were prowling for cocaine and heroin, who were offering their bodies for the price of shooting up with dirty syringes? Morris said that he would tell the kids that every time they went on the streets they were proving themselves to be among life's great losers. Who better to tell the story than Mercury Morris?

Earlier the prosecutor had told the story of Mercury Morris with some force: "He fumbled more than a football game. He fumbled his life away. God gave him a hell of a gift . . . from 1966 to 1975 Mercury truly meant 'Messenger of the Gods.' In 1982 it doesn't. In 1982 it means 'Messenger of dope dealers.'"

Morris's speech from the dock was anguished, filled with regrets for what he had had and what he had thrown away. He had sold two kilos of cocaine to an undercover "narc," one of the Federal Anti-drug Enforcement officers who increasingly attach themselves to the sports–entertainment milieu, where it is known that the cocaine action is fast and somewhat flaunted. The judge spoke softly, addressing Morris by his first name, and the words were spoken softly enough briefly to encourage hope in the man whose hands gripped the rail of the dock more tightly than they had ever held a football. But soon there was iron in the judge's words. Morris had betrayed a society that had given him everything, celebrity, a tremendous lifestyle, in return for his athletic gifts. The thesis was, in fact, not exactly untenable, but the woman judge warmed to it and declared, finally, that Morris would have to pay a price for his betrayal.

Morris was sentenced to twenty years, fifteen of them without the possibility of parole. As the 1980s began to unravel, as it became clear exactly how deeply drug-taking had become part of the American culture, such scenes would become commonplace. John Belushi, a brilliant young comic talent, would die after an orgy of cocaine at a Los Angeles apartment. McKenzie Phillips, gifted daughter of John Phillips of the Mamas and the Papas rock group, would offer Americans the weekly specter of a beautiful young woman succumbing to the ravages of both cocaine and heroin. Eventually, she was written out of her starring role in a television situation comedy. Football players seemed particularly vulnerable.

Carl Eller, a fierce defensive lineman for the Minnesota Vikings, estimated that as many as 40 per cent of all professional players were regular cocaine users. He said that cocaine was the new "Magic Dragon" of sports, adding, "The thing you have to realize, the thing that makes cocaine what it is today in the NFL, is that for players, football players in particular, it duplicates the incredible emotional high they can get on the field. Now a player can get the same thrill from cocaine that he got running 90 yards for a touchdown or making an incredible quarterback sack that saves the game. And they don't actually have to do it any more. They can get the same feeling from the end of a pipe, and all you have to do is have the money for it."

Around the time Mercury Morris was standing trial, an expert on drug abuse was commissioned to write a report on why it was that professional athletes were so highly at risk. He agreed with Eller's Magic Dragon premise and then listed the eight factors that drew the athletes so powerfully toward drug use: the wide availability of cocaine, social pressure to use it, separation from family, lack of supervision, extremely disparate salary levels with stars earning hundreds of thousands of dollars per season, insecurity, boredom and entanglements with women who attach themselves to athletes.

Morris followed a classic pattern. He played an important part in the rise of the Miami Dolphins. Larry Csonka was the running back star, the human battering ram, but Morris was an important element in the Miami backfield. He was quick and strong, and whenever the Dolphins wished to switch the action from Csonka (the surprise value was enormous) Morris was never less than competent and often incisive. But then playing the game was always the simple part.

What was tricky, and increasingly so, was the travel, the four walls of a hotel room and what lay beyond those walls. When a Mercury Morris moved about the lobby of a five-star hotel there was always somebody eager to attach himself (or, more usually, herself) to his celebrity, and often these were people with easy access to the Magic Dragon. There were always people to take away the boredom, nurse an ego, go flying with for a while. Morris earned good money with the Dolphins, and the cost of the first cocaine hits could be carried without strain. But then the Magic Dragon has a tendency to charge compound interest both emotionally and financially. Soon enough Morris's need for cocaine had outstripped his ability to pay. He was perfectly placed to become a dealer, and the suggestion was made to him by his suppliers the moment his credit was exhausted. Morris told the court that he had rehabilitated himself, that he was already working with young people in Florida jails. He said, "These children are charged with adult crimes. I try to give myself as a personal example as to what drugs can do."

Morris was in tears when he was led away from the court-room. Though cocaine was said to have killed 335 Americans in 1981, and to have turned 5 million out of 22 million casual users into addicts, it was hard not to feel twinges of sympathy for Morris, not to see him as victim as well as offender. Certainly, it is true that the game imposes tremendous strains on the individual players, many of whom have grown up in neighbor-hoods where drug-taking and alcohol abuse are endemic. Catapulted into one of the fastest lanes in American life, the football player inevitably faces a period of disorientation. Invariably, he has spent four uneasy years on a university campus, where he has been seen as some kind of physical freak. And always, from high school upwards, football has been discussed in superlatives. When the player eventually establishes himself as a professional, when he becomes a familiar name in newspaper headlines, he is bound to experience some form of let-down. In the long off-season time drags. For many the pace of upward mobility is too fast, and the Magic Dragon happens to be a diversion that has always been wrapped in euphemisms. (For years cocaine has been presented as a recreational drug. Still much of the material of stand-up television comedians is laced with allusions to drug-taking; there is a pervasive sense that it may be wrong, but it sure is fashionable. There was much bleak humor surrounding the incident in which the superb black comedian Richard Pryor came close to burning himself to death while "cooking" cocaine.)

Steve Howe, a pitcher of the Los Angeles Dodgers, was fined $54,000 for slipping back into the cocaine habit after the baseball club had put him through an expensive and much publicized "detoxification" program. The great running back O. J. Simpson sought to provide some perspective when he said, "When I came into the League [in 1968] I saw a lot of drinking, guys really deep into it, and then marijuana came into vogue too. It was macho, it was cool. It was hurting guys' health. It was the thing to do in this country, the macho thing, and it was in all walks of life—Hollywood, sports, everywhere.

"What you're hearing about now in the 1980s goes back to the late 1970s. The whole country seemed to get carried away with it, but now the negative things are coming out and guys are waking up to the dangers. Obviously cocaine is the drug of the affluent, and football sure comes under that category. It's affluence for a short time in a guy's life. But then fame is a fleeting thing. Look at the guys who are involved in the alcohol and drug incidents and you'll find that most of them are not doing anything during the off-season. They're making big money at their sport and nothing else. They have too much time on their hands, too much money. They should be working on the thing they're going to be doing the rest of their lives, doing something constructive away from the field. That's the great problem of too many athletes—too much money, too much empty time. The danger is, you get a false look at yourself and a false look at the world."

A DRAGON FOR WORK BUT NOT FOR FUN

What you also get with football, claims Pete Gent, is an astonishing level of hypocrisy. Gent is a former Dallas Cowboy, a clever occupant of one of the glamor positions, wide receiver.

Gent was fired by the Cowboys because of his liberal and indiscreet use of marijuana. Gent immediately sat down and wrote a best-selling "faction" novel entitled *North Dallas Forty*. At its heart was the contradiction that coaches gave players drugs in order that they could play—and often dangerous drugs—but came down heavily on anyone found to to be using "fun drugs."

Dallas Cowboys general manager Tex Schramm recalls the Pete Gent/*Dallas North Forty* phase with something close to nostalgia; this was especially true in the summer of 1983, when it was revealed that the FBI was probing the alleged drug habits of several of the Cowboy team, including outstanding running back Tony Dorsett. Schramm said, "In those days it was marijuana, not cocaine, and there wasn't any serious crisis. It's always a catastrophe that has to bring something to a head. It's just human nature that it works that way. You go along until something happens and then you do something about it."

Gent argues that the Dallas Cowboys, the entire NFL and all of American society have to accept some of the responsibility for the grim prospect of the nation's most popular game becoming a freak show of the drug culture. "I was pretty amazed at how openly these guys were doing cocaine," says Gent. "They didn't seem to be at all aware of the fact that they were so high-profile and that when they were doing 'coke' in public everybody was watching them. To get into cocaine so openly and so casually and so unconcerned about the consequences—I don't believe they learned that on their own. I believe they learned that playing for an organization that says as long as you win, it's OK. It's just that that's the whole problem of drugs in our culture. It's OK to take a Contac and go to work, and it's OK to take powerful narcotics to play a game. But it's not OK to take 'recreational' drugs. There's no difference between football and society as a whole." Gent also touches a point that gnaws at NFL officials like a particularly severe case of toothache. "That guy selling the $40,000 worth of coke probably knows a gambler. Then you get to where you can't afford the cocaine and he makes you a deal. The clubs don't know what to do. They don't know how to save any of these guys. Who knows who's on what payroll? You can sure run a lot of dollar bills up your nose. It's a wicked drug."

Any suspicion that Gent tends to over-dramatize the problem, gives himself the dramatic license of a highly successful writer, does not survive the weight of evidence that suggests that within football the drug situation is just about out of control. Bill Walsh, the highly imaginative coach who led the San Francisco 49ers to a winning effort in the 1982 Super Bowl, admitted early in 1983 that he was on the point of resigning. The major reason was a sharp increase in drug-taking in the 49er dressing-room. Walsh said that he was considering a move to a general manager's office, where he would be better placed to lead a counter-offensive. "I could look at it from more of a distance," said Walsh. "Let's face it, drugs are prevalent in all forms of our society, at all levels of it . . . at the highest levels, certainly. It would be easy enough to say some drug-ridden team stumbled out on the field in a state of semi-consciousness and couldn't perform, but maybe the other team was the same way. It's not exclusive to the 49ers, and maybe there's less drug use with the 49ers than among teams that will go to the finals of the Super Bowl."

Houston Oilers coach Ed Biles also reported that his team had been deeply hurt by drug use in the short 1982 season. Each week produced a new crop of drug "busts." Drug-enforcement officers hauled Tony Peters, a veteran of Washington Redskins, from training camp in August 1983. The charges had a familiar ring. Peters had made arrangements to sell large amounts of cocaine to two "contacts." One was from the Royal Canadian Mounted Police; the other was a Federal narc.

A few days before Peters's arrest, NFL commissioner Pete Rozelle announced the four-game suspension of four players, Ross Browner and Pete Johnson of the Cincinnati Bengals, E. J. Junior of the St Louis Cardinals and Greg Stemrick of the New Orleans Saints. Rozelle said that he hoped this action would serve as a deterrent to other drug-users in the League. He was no longer saying the League had a "small problem." Yet, according to Rozelle, resolute action on the part of the NFL, the individual clubs and the players' union would first contain the trouble, then wipe it away. It seemed, at the very best, a pious hope.

Pete Gent was right when he claimed that the game's problem was also society's, but he omitted to say that nowhere in American life are men more imbued with the need to succeed than in professional football. The game provides its own Magic Dragon—the roar of the crowd, the violence, the sense of living by the minute. It also creates an ambience in which reality is suspended as long as a football player can do his job, as long as his nerve and his body hold. While this happens the Magic Dragon flies beautifully, but the return to earth can be brutal.

The suspicion is that Rozelle misses the point when he talks about deterrents. He should perhaps look more closely at the causes rather than at possible antidotes. He should look at the morality of football, its relentless dismissal of human values. Football needs to humanize itself before it can begin to think in terms of improving on the behavior patterns of the rest of America.

Football expects the athletic elite of every generation to go to war over a few places in the professional game. It says that disillusionment and physical suffering will always be the yield for most of the contenders. This being so, it has to accept that the Magic Dragon will continue to fly over every scrimmage.

8

Soldier-Priests

A few minutes after the end of each year's Super Bowl there is a ritual. A telephone rings in the dressing-room of the winners, and over the clatter of celebration there is a shout of special urgency. It announces that Washington is on the line. The President is calling. The ensuing conversation, picked up by television and relayed across the nation, is invariably remarkable for the deference displayed by the chief executive of the most powerful nation on earth toward a coach of football players.

It is as though the President has been relegated by the drama of the game to the role of awed onlooker, someone grateful to make contact with the conqueror of the day on which all of America's competitive instincts become inflamed. Sometimes this seems to be more than an illusion created by the drumbeats and huckstering of television. It is certainly true that at the height of the Watergate crisis President Richard Nixon confided that he envied no man more than the coach of Washington Redskins. Partly he was reflecting his own desperate circumstances; partly he was underlining the universal American respect for the institution of football coach.

The football coach has become much more than another functionary of sport. He is expected to embody the very deepest of Americans' perceptions of themselves. He is expected to be authoritative, tough but fair, philosophical but imbued with a hunger for action. Ideally, he is a soldier-priest.

No coach met this ideal more perfectly than Vince Lombardi, at least in his own lifetime and in his public persona. The record books of the NFL tell an extraordinary story of Lombardi's success, but they fail to cover fully the range of his influence or the degree of his intensity. He once berated his wife for ignoring his general advice to a team banquet and taking a particularly calorific dessert. But such quirks did nothing to sully the purity of his image. Lombardi turned a wretched Green Bay Packers team into one of the most formidable forces in the history of the game. In the process, many claimed, he instructed a generation of Americans in how to think.

Lombardi's famous declaration, "Winning isn't everything. It's the only thing," became an article of American faith. It was something to place alongside the statue of the Marines at Iwo Jima. He confessed that the idea of defeat caused him physical nausea, and he said, "Coaches who can outline plays on a blackboard are a dime a dozen. The ones who win get inside their players and motivate." One of his players, tackle Henry Jordan observed drily, "He treats us all the same—like dogs."

Lombardi was 46 years old when he took over the team of Green Bay, a small town near Milwaukee, Wisconsin, in 1959. The club had known better days. It was disheveled and near-bankrupt, and it had won just one of twelve games the previous season. Lombardi, a bull-like figure with short-cropped black hair and broad face framed by horn-rimmed spectacles, announced at his first team meeting, "I have never been on a losing team, gentlemen, and I don't intend to start now."

In his first year, with only minor adjustments to team personnel, Lombardi won seven of twelve games. In the following year he carried the western conference of the NFL, losing to Philadelphia Eagles in the title game, and he was clearly embarked upon some empire-building. The Packers won the title in 1961, 1962, 1965, 1966 and 1967 and swept the first two Super Bowls.

Packer power was built on sound military principles. Lombardi was the son of Italian immigrants, growing up in the Sheepshead Bay section of Brooklyn, where his father was a butcher. Vince Lombardi was a gifted student, a classic first-generation American seeking to extend his parents' hard-won bridgehead on the new continent of hope. He won scholarships to Fordham University, where he acquired an honors degree and a fierce reputation on the football field. He played guard on an offensive line known as the "Seven Blocks of Granite." He had a year in law school, played some minor-league football, then taught chemistry, algebra and Latin at a New Jersey high school. In his spare time he coached the football team.

He spent seven years at the high school, weighing the qualities of American youth, determining their strengths, speculating on ways to remove their weaknesses. After a brief return to his old university, he moved to the West Point Military Academy. It was at West Point that Lombardi learned the lessons that would shape his thinking. At West Point, under the guidance of the fierce disciplinarian Colonel Earl Blaik, Lombardi appreciated the value of power, controlled, skillfully deployed power. It was the single most pervasive influence on the man whom many consider the most committed football coach of all time. He always said that victory came not only with thorough organization, a clear chain of command, but also with an almost mystical self-belief.

According to Lombardi, it was not enough to merely scorn the idea of defeat. It was necessary to reject it totally, as you might something actively injurious to your health. He would make gods of players who displayed, beyond their talent, a special need to win. Paul Hornung was such a player. Hornung, blond, versatile, absolutely committed to Lombardi and the Packers, was murderously efficient near an opponent's line. Lombardi's face would glow when he spoke of him. "You have to know what Hornung means to his team," said Lombardi. "In the middle of the field he may be only slightly better than an average ball player, but inside the 20-yard line he is one of the greatest I have ever seen. He smells the goal line." Before he was suspended for a year for betting on games, Hornung became almost an extension of Lombardi's deepest instincts for the game. In 1961, when the resurrected Packers demolished the New York Giants in the NFL championship game, Hornung was immense. He broke a play-off record with 19 points. Lombardi . . . Hornung: one defined the American hero; the other showed that the specifications could be met.

It was a time of American renewal after the sleepy days of Eisenhower. John F. Kennedy was preaching to Americans about the value of self-sacrifice, directing them toward heroism. And off into space they went, square-jawed, eyes shining with idealism. Lombardi expressed the mood on the football field. Win, said Lombardi. Win for your school, your college, your pro team, your country, yourself. Win and keep winning. Hollywood offered John Wayne. Football offered Vince Lombardi. For a long time the conventional view was that Lombardi was a glorious expression of the very best of American life.

It was nearly twenty years later that someone suggested that Vince Lombardi may have got it wrong, that rather than lifting American youth to new levels of achievement, he may well have perverted it.

Dr Tutko, the sports psychologist, made this astounding claim to a sub-committee of the House of Representatives in Washington in 1980. He told the Congressmen that violence had become institutionalized in American sport and that generations of young people had come to believe that their only moral imperative was to win. He said that it was a sickness most visible in the ranks of professional football, the nation's most popular game. And he added, "It goes back to Lombardi and his famous statement that winning isn't everything. Anyone casually watching professional sport over the last few years would know that this attitude has got into professional sport so deeply it probably will never be removed. But if people think this is alarming they should look at the high school fields. They should see that the violence is a kind of infectious disease, often transmitted by the coaches.

"In his time Lombardi was a unifying force in this country, emphasizing splendid virtues of determination, of refusing to quit, of winning through, come what may. But the country has changed, and Lombardi's emphasis has been taken into a different context, and now it is vicious and sick."

A VICIOUS CHALLENGE TO A CIVILIZED SOCIETY

Tutko was in Washington to support a Bill aimed at making a criminal offense of any act of violence on the sports field. The sponsoring congressman, Democrat William Mottl, said in the Congress, "The Bill is directed toward the kind of vicious, dangerous contact that a civilized society should brand as criminal whether it occurs inside or outside the sports arena— conduct in which a player actually steps outside the role of athlete and sportsman."

Tutko said that he was in Washington not in any hope of reforming the professional game but rather to try to draw attention to the sinister influence that it was exerting on American youth. He said, "Yes, I do despair of the professional game. Violence has become institutionalized and there is no way of displacing its hold on the pros. It is reinforced by the appetite of the public. They pay big bucks for the violence. Football people may tell you about the skills and the beauty of the game, and we know they exist, but don't let's kid ourselves: most people go to a football game for the violence.

"Knocking the quarterback's head off is a means to an end among the pros, and we have to look at the kids now. It is alarming to watch the game at the 12-year-old level. The coach tells the kids to 'Stick it to 'em' and he doesn't seem to know what he is doing in psychological terms. What we are doing is creating an unhealthy environment for our kids."

Lombardi, who died from cancer in 1970, would no doubt have been bemused by the arguments in Washington. He would have said, as his defenders did, hotly, that he was seeking to enhance rather than corrupt, to set levels of determination and performance without which the highest goals facing young men and nations could never be achieved. What was wrong with glorifying the power and the ambition of a Paul Hornung? Was he not something to celebrate as he churned toward the line? Was power—power in the cause of right, of course—not the supreme American virtue? Tutko's case was that Lombardi's emphasis, perhaps innocently devised, had created a moral vacuum. According to Lombardi, Tutko argued, victory had to be won whatever the cost. You knocked the quarterback's head off, or at least tried to earnestly. Life was messy, hard. You had to inflict yourself. It might not be pretty, but there was a job to do. Lombardi said that defeat was a disease, infectious and unAmerican. He cleansed himself of germs, and his teams kept winning.

In ten seasons Lombardi won ninety-six NFL games, lost thirty-four and had six ties. After winning his second Super Bowl in 1968 he retired from the touchline. He left as the Caesar of football.

After just one year he was back, shouting, exhorting, asking for one more push, one more grapple with the specter of defeat. Washington Redskins had lured him back to the touchline. The Redskins were as hapless as the Packers a decade earlier. In fourteen years the Washington club had not had one winning season. But again Lombardi tinkered with a demoralized team, lifted its sights, projected its victories. In his first year the Redskins won seven games, lost five and tied two. Americans settled in their armchairs or on the stools of their favorite bars, turned on their television sets and waited for another Lombardi epic. Lombardi could be depended upon. He had the track record. He had defined what it was to be a winner.

The doctors said that the cancer that killed Vince Lombardi

was of a particularly virulent type. The reaction to his death was one of deep shock. An idea, as much as a celebrity, had fallen.

If Lombardi would have been bemused by the Washington hearings, he would have been dumbfounded by the press conference called by the Philadelphia Eagles in 1982. Dick Vermeil, a blond, powerfully built 46-year-old, told the gathering that he was retiring as head coach of the Eagles, ironically at the age at which Lombardi had taken over the Green Bay Packers. As Vermeil spoke, tears rolled down his cheeks. The television cameras whirred. He said that he was "burned out." Vermeil had taken the Eagles to the 1981 Super Bowl in the New Orleans Superdome. The Eagles had been outplayed by a more relaxed Raiders team. Vermeil admitted that in his own mind the game had become a monster, endlessly demanding of his time and his every thought. Rival coaches admitted that Vermeil was a worker, but some suggested that maybe he talked about work a little too much. Hard work, indeed total immersion, was a condition of the job. It was common knowledge that Vermeil had taken to sleeping in his office overnight. It meant that he avoided the commuter traffic congealing on the bridges and freeways of Philadelphia. It meant that he had more time to analyze films.

A heavily emotional man, Vermeil had carried the intensity of Lombardi into a more sophisticated age. When a player executed a move perfectly, Vermeil would rush to embrace him. When a play broke down, it seemed that Vermeil trembled on the brink of disaster, a great personal defeat. He lived suspended between heaven and hell. He wanted to win as desperately as any man since Lombardi, but the odds against such success had grown with the billion-dollar television contracts and the sense that to carry a Super Bowl was to carry the nation. Vermeil was widely respected throughout the League. His tactical sense was acute. But he couldn't live with the idea of being second. The shame of it drove him away.

By 1983 even *Pro!*, a house organ of the NFL, was admitting that pressures within the game had reached disturbing levels. At the start of a piece headlined "Feeling the pressure," *Pro!* ran this mock job ad: "HELP WANTED—Dynamic executive to fill high-level position. Extremely long hours. Almost no opportunity for promotion. Responsible for minimum of 45 employees around the clock. Skill in public relations area, i.e. press conferences, radio and television shows. Must possess technical knowledge above reproach. Must be willing to take blame. Directly responsible to owner and millions of customers. Salary may be less than some employees you supervise. Only 28 clubs available nationwide at one time. Send references and résumé to PO Box NFL. Weak of heart need not apply."

Art Rooney, the aging founder of the Pittsburgh Steelers, agreed that the coach's job had changed profoundly through the 1960s and the 1970s. "In the old days," said Rooney, "the owners and the coaches would sit around and talk for hours. You'd ride the train together, you'd drink together. It was just different. The press used to sit at the table with you on draft day. Heck, they wanted you to win as much as you did. I hired Walt Kiesling to coach our team three different times, which meant I had to rehire him twice. There would be too many people hollering if an owner hired the same man back today. And I'll tell you another thing. If we stayed up till 3 a.m. in those days, it usually meant we all were together in some hotel bar."

Psychologist Bruce Ogilvie suggests that the modern football coach faces a challenge that ultimately cannot be met. In a sense, cancer probably saved Lombardi's football reputation, or at least preserved it as a shining monument, even as it so cruelly devoured his body. It removed from him the possibility of defeat, the erosion of his image of invincibility. Ogilvie says, "All these men [football coaches in the NFL] are fully expected to create excellence on demand. And they are so much more visible than other professional executives. The question is: How long can a man stand the assault of fans, the community and the media? Injuries and the money today's athletes make add more stress to an already stressful situation. It's hard to blame the owners. It really is. The owner has to feed the public, and he has to feed them the skin of the head coach sometimes.

"The head coach is expected to be all-knowing, a great healer, a perfect individual on and off the field. We still don't understand why some coaches exhibit more staying power, psychologically, than others. It has something to do with their value systems. Family, religion, other things all enter into that."

But mostly, perhaps, it is the set of values that Lombardi defined on the touchline of Green Bay. The need to win is, of course, basic to professional sport, but in American football it has been stressed as nowhere else. A wealthy businessman toying with the idea of buying a franchise of the North American Soccer League expressed it quite well when he was told that in England many League games end in a tie. "No," he was told, "there are no overtimes, double overtimes." He was nonplussed. He said, "Hell, a tied game is about as much fun as kissing your sister."

IN FALL 1982, SOME DEGREE OF MAYHEM

In the NFL regular season ties do occur from time to time, but they are considered an abomination. A tie is better than a loss, but not by much. Such thinking has always brought pressure on the head coach, even in Art Rooney's more amiable days of Pullman cars and tinkling whiskey glasses. But in the fall of 1982 it had to be said that there was a degree of mayhem.

Eight of the NFL's twenty-eight coaches were cleaning out their offices. Four of them—Leeman Bennett of the Atlanta Falcons, Jack Patera of the Seattle Seahawks, Marv Levy of the Kansas City Chiefs, and Ray Malavesi of the Los Angeles Rams—were fired. All of them went angrily, arguing that the owners had simply lacked patience. Another year would have done it, they said. Another year would have seen flames licking around the offense, steel in the defense. They all seemed to believe it. Of the other departures, Walt Michaels of the New York Jets officially retired, though some were questioning his equilibrium even before the Jets were removed from the 1982 play-offs by the Miami Dolphins. After an earlier game against the Los Angeles (formerly Oakland) Raiders, Michaels claimed that he had been called away from a vital team talk at half-time to take a call from his club owner. Michaels claimed that it had been a ruse by rival owner Al Davis, a man with a reputation for unscrupulous behavior. In fact, the call was made by a barman in Long Island anxious to make a contribution to the team's game plan. Michaels, who was voted American Football Conference Coach of the Year four years earlier, appeared to be losing his grip.

Chuck Knox, a brilliant success in Los Angeles with the Rams but a man who suffered hard times in Buffalo, shuffled west to replace Patera in Seattle; Vermeil had his public "burn-out," and New York Giants' Ray Perkins decided to take up the vacancy of head coach at the University of Alabama.

Superficially, it might have seemed that Perkins was stepping out of the peculiar pressure chamber of professional sport in New York City. The New York fans, perhaps the least tolerant of failure in the Western world, had become impatient with the dour Southerner. A native of Mississippi, Perkins had been a star wide receiver for Alabama under the legendary head coach Paul "Bear" Bryant. The truth was that in some ways Perkins was accepting the greatest pressure of his life. He was also providing evidence that football coaches have a romantic tendency that often outstrips good sense. There was no doubt that the pressures in the big stadium in Birmingham, Alabama, would be quite as intense as those in the huge Giants stadium in the New Jersey meadowlands, which is just a short drive from Manhattan via the Lincoln Tunnel. Perkins was taking over more than a job in Alabama. He was seeking to replace a man who in his own world had come as close as anyone to the scale of a Vince Lombardi.

The point was underlined just a few days after Perkins took up his new duties. Bryant collapsed and died just a few days into his retirement. He was fulfilling a prophecy. He had always said that he feared a future without football. Tall, craggy-faced, "The Bear" was one of the great institutions, perhaps the greatest, of the college game. His "Crimson Tide" team had set daunting standards. Throughout the state of Alabama flags were flown at half-mast. With tears in his eyes, the Governor called for a day of mourning for the coach.

In his youth Bryant was as implacable as the mature Lombardi. He once recalled that while coaching in Texas he had his players slaving on the practice field in 100+° temperatures. Several players fainted. Bryant had been standing on top of an observation tower, bullhorn in his hand. For the first time he considered the fact that there were perhaps limits beyond which football coaches should not go. Bryant mellowed, adjusted to the new generations and the climate of the times, which insisted that Alabama should use black players. Alabama would produce a line of brilliant white quarterbacks right into the 1980s, but soon enough the power positions would be occupied almost exclusively by blacks.

Bryant was a pragmatist, a winner and a figure of vast

authority as he walked from the field in Birmingham. Always he was flanked by state troopers in their 10-gallon hats. Always he was mobbed. He was the nearest thing to a pontiff of the gridiron. It was commonly agreed that had he ever run for the governorship of Alabama, he would have won by a landslide, and had he gone for the presidency, there is not much doubt that he would have at least carried the South.

Perkins's new post offered a formidable challenge indeed; perhaps only one other college appointment in North America carried a heavier obligation to produce a winning team, and that was the one that Gerry Faust, a devout, middle-aged Roman Catholic, accepted early in 1981. Faust took over as head coach of Notre Dame, where coach Knute Rockne made winning for the college a kind of sacred tryst with destiny.

Notre Dame is a university in South Bend, Indiana, an ivy-covered, red-brick place that has good enough educational credentials but whose heartbeat is truly registered only on the football field. Local residents refer to the university, a shade ironically, as "Touchdown Jesus."

Faust was a controversial appointment. His previous success had come at the high school level. In eighteen years at Moeller High, a Catholic school in the suburbs of Cincinnati, Ohio, Faust compiled a record of 174 wins, seventeen defeats and two ties. These were staggering statistics even when set against the fact that Faust had a supporting staff of eighteen coaches. Moeller had more than two coaches for every day of the week. They included a kicking coach, a defensive back coach, a special teams coach, an offensive line coach, a defensive line coach, a running back coach, a quarterback coach, a linebacker coach, a conditioning coach. There was also Faust, a praying coach. Many of the university's fiercely loyal graduates were concerned by Faust's lack of experience at the college level. Others were perturbed, even alarmed, by his heavy and very public piety.

He made no secret of his practice of getting the entire Moeller football squad to kneel before a grotto of Our Lady and pray for victory. He also owned up to authorizing this sign in the dressing-room: "God is like Bayer Aspirin—He works wonders. God is like Ford—He's got a better idea. God is like Dial—He gives you round-the-clock protection. God is like Coke—He's the Real Thing. God is like Hallmark Cards—He cares enough to send the very best."

Notre Dame's athletic director, Roger Valdiserri, was some-what aghast that Faust was in the running for the job. He said, "If Faust gets the job, I'm going to have to sit him down and talk this over." Valdiserri was perhaps mindful of the fact that just a few years earlier the walls of Touchdown Jesus had shuddered to the revelation that certain football players had been smuggling girls into the dormitories. After his talk with Valdiserri, Faust, a man of much charm despite his zeal, said, "Yes, it has been suggested I might change my style a little bit, but there is no way I'll do that. My feeling is that if you cannot say a prayer at Notre Dame, where can you? I came here to do a job, not change myself. I won't thrust religion down the guys' throats. I'll remind them of its value, though, and they'll have a chance to join me in prayer.

"It would be foolish not to recognize that I'm dealing with older people, but some values are the same, however old you get. I've always believed in character above everything else, and already I've seen some new candidates for Notre Dame, and we're talking about young men of the highest character. But who doesn't benefit from the value of prayer? Maybe it is my way of saying that there are other things apart from football. No, I don't believe the pressures are too great for young players. I ask only that these young men bring to football the qualities they have to show in the exam room. The prayer I ask for is only that we do things to the best of our ability. I do not say that we should pray to win. No, no, that would be wrong.

"I've dreamed of coaching Notre Dame. The idea of it has always fascinated me, excited me . . . but there are some things I wouldn't sacrifice even for this honor. On top of the list is the ability to be myself. Try to be something you're not and you're finished. Then you don't do anything."

SLAVES OF A LESSER GOD

Ideally, the coach represents authority, fair but unyielding on certain basic principles. Faust's religiosity may seem extreme, and certainly it led to his being considered an eccentric in the hard-bitten school of college coaches, but for many people outside the game the oddity and, perhaps, the appeal of Faust is that he has not been sucked in completely by the rituals and the

dubious moralities of football. To a great many coaches, to a
Lombardi and a Vermeil certainly, there is no doubt that the
game can become God. Vermeil's zeal was built into his
character at an early stage. Before the 1981 Super Bowl, his
eldest brother said, "When Dick was in college he would get up
for an 8 a.m. class, be in school until 4 p.m., work from then until
midnight in Dad's auto mechanic shop, study until 3 a.m., then
get up at 7 a.m. and start all over again. He developed an ability
to push on."

One of Vermeil's players, Philadelphia tight end Keith
Krepfle, added, "He tore us down mentally and physically and
then he built us up together. We all had the common experience
of hard work. And Dick worked harder than anybody."

There is something unnaturally relentless about the American
concept of the coach's job. It is almost a parody of the notion
that the successful man of business or industry spends the best
years of his life working twelve hours a day, makes his mark,
pays his insurance premiums, has a few soft years drinking
martinis at the country club, then has a heart attack, thus
allowing his widow to sell up and move to Florida. Certainly, the
disillusionment of Dick Vermeil seemed profound enough when
he announced that he had nothing more to give the Philadelphia
Eagles, that he had one morning gone to the well and found that
it was dry.

Sometimes it does happen that a successful coach can step
beyond the prototype, can create for himself a life apart from the
touchline and the locker room. But it is a rarity, almost a
sublime act of defiance against the strictures of a somewhat
crazed world. No one has pulled off the trick more satisfactorily,
at less cost to his reputation as a football coach, than Chuck
Noll, general of the Pittsburgh Steelers.

A powerfully built, taciturn man, Noll once shocked
Pittsburgh club officials by turning down an invitation to a high-
powered seminar on man management in football. He told them,
"No, thanks. I've planned to do a little scuba diving." He also
raised some eyebrows when he revealed that he had season
tickets for the local symphony orchestra, rum behavior indeed
for a gridiron man. Other bizarre conduct included the possession of a pilot's license and a habit of turning up for the team
flight armed with the works of Kafka and Kierkegaard.

Noll explains that he learned early that football can easily dominate a man's life. He resolved to give only so much of himself. He would let a little light into the football. He needed the sustenance of family, music, the splendid calm of deep blue water and the exhilaration of nosing a Cherokee through the clouds.

Noll graduated from college in Dayton, Ohio, then played seven seasons for the brilliant Paul Brown at Cleveland. As a player, Noll displayed a well rounded character. He performed as a guard for three seasons, a linebacker for four. Guards are stoic characters; shorn of all glamor, guards are big men with light feet, who resist the rush of the defensive line that seeks to wreck the quarterback. A broken quarterback is the ultimate reproach for a guard. For the linebacker it is the ultimate triumph. A linebacker is a hero, a marauder, mean and fast, a seeker and a destroyer. Remarkably, Noll pulled off both assignments with great aplomb. Nor did he panic when, in his first year as a professional coach, his Steelers lost thirteen games. He said coolly that he had seen how much work there was to do in Pittsburgh and that if the club had the patience, so did he.

Pittsburgh's patience was rewarded marvelously. Noll carried the Super Bowl in 1977, 1978, 1979, and 1980. The Steelers did more than win trophies. They set standards. The Dallas Cowboys like to describe themselves as America's team. But it is an illusion, another reflection of Texan hubris. In the 1970s Noll's Steelers, like Lombardi's Packers a decade earlier, proved that they were a serious football team. They were real.

Noll still has Jack Lambert at middle linebacker. Middle linebacker is captain of the defense. Lambert is a man of quite awesome ferocity. When the Steelers marched to their fourth successive Super Bowl in 1980, subduing a fine Los Angeles Rams effort in the Pasadena Rose Bowl, Lambert elicited a rare flash of emotion from Noll, who embraced the fiercest of his warriors at the end of the game. It seemed to many that Lambert had started the game with the express intention of individually dismantling the Los Angeles team. Most agreed that he had come honorably close to fulfilling his ambition completely. Lambert was just one example of excellence. The offensive line was given superb leadership by center Mike Webster, still arguably the best man in the League in this difficult, often unheralded role. Alongside Webster were men accomplished in every aspect of the trade, men like offensive tackle Larry Brown and offensive guard Sam Davis. We have talked already of the power of Franco Harris and the wit, speed and grace of Lynn Swann and John Stallworth. There was too the thundering menace of defensive end Mean Joe Greene, 6 feet 4 inches, a man who could produce at a second's notice the purest of hostility.

And there was Noll's lieutenant and field commander, Terry Bradshaw. The boy from Louisiana always had a wonderfully strong right arm, but there were some who thought that he would never be mentally tough enough for the National Football League. When Bradshaw threw into the arms of an opponent, the crowd at Three Rivers Stadium howled for his blood, and even some of Noll's coaching assistants wondered if the quarterback had enough of the right stuff.

Noll was moved neither by the howls nor the doubts. He said, "Bradshaw's my quarterback. Bradshaw can do the job, and as long as I'm coach here, he will." There was no compromise from Noll. He even rejected pleas that he should at least tell Bradshaw which plays to use in specific circumstances.

Ed Kiley, a Steeler official, recalls, "There was a hell of a lot of pressure on Chuck. The word kept coming from upstairs, 'Send in some plays.' The feeling was that Bradshaw was dumb and it was time the coach did something about it. Chuck never blinked. He said Bradshaw was his quarterback. He had a good arm and a good brain. All he needed was time to work it out. They kept at Chuck, but there was never a question that he would quit on Bradshaw calling the plays. He won a lot of respect in the locker-room."

Of course, there are other coaches who have achieved detachment, a certain dignity beyond the game. But few have seemed to arrive at it as naturally, as instinctively, as Chuck Noll. It took a personal tragedy for Sam Rutigliano, coach of the Cleveland Browns, to see that he had been immersing himself too deeply in the game. His daughter died in a car crash. He thought bitterly of how many hours had been spent away from home agonizing over games, the results of which seemed irrelevant now. He determined that he too would keep a little back from the game.

THREE GIANTS . . . AND A LITTLE SPACE

When John Giles, the former Leeds United and Republic of Ireland soccer international, moved to North America to play and coach his game in Philadelphia and Vancouver, he was at first fascinated, then appalled, at the extent of the football coach's responsibility. "It seems a little bit unreal to me," said Giles. "I mean, that one man should have such vast influence over the course of a game. If one move fails, he selects another and then another. He is totally in charge of his team's operation. Football players are obviously superb athletes but what happens to their spontaneity, which to me is the essence of sport? I find it very unnatural. I don't really feel sport should be something so mechanical.

"For me, the beauty of soccer, the reason why I think it is the best team game of all, is that there are so many factors outside the control of a coach. If a coach could control a soccer game, it would be very boring indeed. In American football the play becomes just an extension of the will and imagination of the two coaches. This can be fascinating, sure, but I'm not certain it has much to do with sport, certainly as Europeans know sport."

It is true that football is like no other game and that the demands on its coaches are similarly unique. Noll, as we have said, has perhaps had most success in meeting the challenge of producing a winning football record and a life for himself and his family which does not hang on the weekend score. Of Noll's contemporaries, three names tower above the rest: those of Don Shula, Tom Landry and Bud Grant. All three of them share intensity. All suggest that football occupies the dead center of their existence. But they have all stayed the long course without a hint of burn-out.

Shula played defensive back for Cleveland, Baltimore and Washington and took over as head coach of Baltimore at the remarkably early age of 32. He was a source of much controversy when he left Baltimore for Miami in 1969, the League ordering his new club to give up its number one draft choice as the penalty for "tampering" with the employee of a rival. For Miami it was the best of deals. Within three years Shula had created the NFL's perfect season, Miami winning all seventeen games on the way to carrying off Super Bowl VII. A tall, handsome man,

Shula declared, "This is the greatest moment in my coaching life. We can let the record speak for itself." *Time* magazine lauded Shula as "perhaps the soundest, best organized technical mind in pro football today." Shula tends to be embarrassed by such accolades, dismisses them with a groan and a downward glance. He has said, "I'm about as subtle as a punch in the mouth. I'm just a guy who rolls up his sleeves and goes to work."

At 59, Tom Landry is the doyen of NFL coaches. A Second World War flier with the Eighth Air Force—he is credited with thirty missions—Landry, like Noll and Shula, often displays a sense of a wider world beyond the gridiron. On the touchline he has been known to show concern and satisfaction but none of the pyrotechnics so hungrily sought by the television networks.

As a player, Landry won attention as a sound defensive back for the New York Giants, and in 1960 he moved home to Texas as the first head coach of the new franchise, Dallas Cowboys. Landry's patient work, in which he stressed defensive discipline and developed the now common 4–3 defensive line formation, turned a fragile club into Super Bowl winners. Dallas's consistency, their inevitable presence in the play-off games, earned them in some quarters the title of "America's team," though, as we have noted, it was one much disputed by the blue-collar workers of Green Bay and Pittsburgh in particular. Landry established a placid style. A devout Methodist, he took some of the grandeur away from the coach's room. He once said, "If a team has character, it doesn't need stimulation."

Bud Grant of the Minnesota Vikings is a droll character, as you would imagine from the formula he once offered to aspiring coaches. "A good coach," said Grant, "needs a patient wife, a loyal dog and a great quarterback, but not necessarily in that order." Grant created a powerful tradition in Minnesota with the same tactical emphasis as that of his great rivals. He believed in hard, relentless defense. In the late 1960s Grant's defensive line was known as the "Purple People Eaters." When the Vikings reached the 1970 Super Bowl, Grant said, "We don't win with mirrors or gimmicks. There are no short cuts. You win with hard work and good players."

Noll, Shula, Landry and Grant might be said to be the survivors, the men who have seen football for what it is. They have observed that it offers glory and romance but that at its heart is much savagery. They have been wise. They have kept their distance.

John Madden showed another kind of wisdom. He, too, saw the savagery. But he also knew that he was incapable of preventing himself from being drawn into the center of it. As a brilliant, hard-driving coach of the Oakland Raiders, he would rage on the touch-line. He had great success with the Raiders, but he knew he was operating on a short fuse. He left for a successful career with CBS television. He told the *Pro!* probe into coaching pressures, "I believe there are two types of person-alities. The 'A' personality worries too much about things that he can't control. I was an 'A' in Oakland. That's why I had to get out. Dick Vermeil was an 'A.' I believe the 'A's can last ten years—maximum.

"The 'B' personality is the opposite. Landry, Shula, Grant and Noll come to mind. Shula was an 'A' who learned to be a 'B.' I remember before a game in Dallas one Saturday Tony Dorsett had checked into the hospital with chest pains. I asked Landry what he was going to do. He said that he would talk to Tony the next day and see how he felt. I was shocked. I would have called the hospital a hundred times already to get a doctor's report."

Joe Gibbs, Washington's coach and a 1983 Super Bowl winner, confides, "I change in six months [of the season]. My blood pressure goes up. My heart rate goes up. In July I've been running and playing racquetball. I feel good." Joe Gibbs is 42.

Landry, for one, is generous toward some of his younger rivals. If they seem obsessive, haunted by all kinds of demons, he points out that in his first five years at Dallas he failed to achieve a winning season and that an owner couldn't display such patience today. The local press would turn ugly. The fans, inflamed and able to watch winning teams on their television screens each weekend would bay for blood. The coach, whatever his knowledge, however surely he could point to a breakthrough next fall, would go. It is interesting that since Pittsburgh's last triumph in the 1980 Super Bowl, there has been no hint of the growth of a new dynasty. Oakland Raiders won in 1981 but were unable to mount similar efforts in 1982 and 1983. San Francisco, winners in 1982, had a disastrous time when the new season opened. In January 1983 the Washington Redskins, thrust forward by the running power of John Riggins, overwhelmed

Shula's Dolphins in Pasadena. In the opening game in September 1983 the Redskins wilted under pressure from Landry's Cowboys. And so the pressure goes, up and down the League. There is no cover, nowhere to relax.

In the 1950s and 1960s and on into the early 1970s Paul Brown was able to create for himself some space and some time, first in Cleveland with the Browns, then with the Cincinnati Bengals. In the process Brown took the job of professional coach as first defined by George Halas in Chicago and refined it to the point where it is today, which is to say that it requires about eighteen hours of each day, including Sunday.

It was Brown who first insisted on calling the plays from the touchline. He presented his players with playbooks, detailed expositions of every aspect of the team's game plan. It was the product of a dictatorial mind, and the weight of it could be supported only by winning football. Brown produced it consistently for Cleveland, then reproduced his touch at Cincinnati. He said that a coach should be masterful, and he proved that it was possible. He made it hard on the men who followed.

John Madden, who walked away from the game because he sensed that within it were the seeds of his own destruction, was commentating on a televised game between New York Giants and Los Angeles Rams in the fall of 1983. It was a close game, crucial for both clubs. After indifferent seasons, Los Angeles and New York had appointed new coaches. Late in the fourth quarter, when it was clear that Los Angeles would win, Madden asked that the cameras dwell for a second or two on the touchline, where the new coach, John Robinson, stood. Robinson, a protégé of Madden and former coach of the University of Southern California, was surrounded by players and assistant coaches. In a tight group about twenty men urged on the Los Angeles defensive unit. Madden then asked the cameras to switch to the opposite touchline. Bill Parcels, the Giants' new man, was wearing the kind of expression that you tend to see on the face of a victim of a road smash. He was standing quite alone.

"There you have it," said Madden with a sigh. "There's the whole ball of wax. There's the coaching job."

9

War in the Air

Now that the sun has set on the career of Lynn Swann and is slanting low over that of his Pittsburgh partner John Stallworth, there are no clear claimants to the mastery of the air, of the graceful but intensely athletic art of receiving the football. But if you were a coach who needed a touchdown to win the game and there were just a few seconds on the clock, or if you were a quarterback with cold hands and a sweating brow, you would not complain if your only option was to throw to James Lofton.

If Lofton played for the Dallas Cowboys or the San Diego Chargers, there is no doubt that he would already be part of the legend of the game. Lofton is 27 years old. He is 6 feet 3 inches tall, a trim 182 pounds, and he covers 40 yards in roughly 4.4 seconds. More impressive, though, is his ability to climb into the air and hang there, arms outstretched, hands dry, adroit, sometimes even magnetic, it seems. Unfortunately for his place in the history books, Lofton plays for Green Bay Packers, who have gone down a long way from the days of Lombardi and before that coach Curly Lambeau, for whom the Green Bay Stadium is named. It is not only that Green Bay lack some of the tools to make a good receiver great, an offensive line that can offer solid protection to the quarterback and a quarterback who is mobile enough to win the extra second in which a defensive cover can be broken; Green Bay often also seem to commit a terrible sin of omission. They appear to undervalue Lofton's superb range of physical gifts, and this is even more incomprehensible in light of the fact that his fellow members of the receiving unit, the seasoned John Jefferson and Paul Coffman, are both first-rate decoys and more than capable of delivering their own killing strokes.

Jefferson and Coffman are trustworthy receivers who can, from time to time, reach out for something special. Lofton announces his talent with almost every movement. He is a corner back's nightmare. At the best of times playing corner back is a thankless job. Offensive linemen complain about their anonymity, but when things go wrong it is a blessing. When things go wrong for a corner back, they happen in the white light of the very center of the action. A corner back has duties beyond the marking of a receiver. If the opposing team elects to run the ball, he has to link with the linebackers and the safeties as they peel away the blockers and hit the man cradling the ball. But it is when the quarterback throws the ball that the corner back is poised between doing his job competently and hell.

Leon Bright is an amiable young man who hails from a poor township in the swamp country of Florida. He currently plays in the suicide alley of the New York Giants special teams. Special teams return and block for kick-off and punt returns, cover kick-offs and field goal attempts. It is risky, arduous work, its chief benefit being that it offers fringe players the chance to catch the attention of the coach. Playing on a special team is better than being out of the action, better certainly than pumping gas or working in a hamburger joint, but it is bottom-of-the-line work in the NFL. However, Bright much prefers the special teams to playing corner back. A few years ago Bright was briefly converted from wide receiver to corner back by the British Columbia Lions of the Canadian Football League. I recall talking with him in his room after a day of training camp. Bright was in a state of shock.

"That's a hell of a job I've been given," said Bright. "It's so unnatural, you know? You're running backwards most of the time. You've got to try to give the guy a good hit, but you can't afford a penalty. You're walking on ice. Man, there's some tension out there. When I played wide receiver I didn't realize what an advantage I had. I was facing forward. The other guy didn't know which way I was going to go. Everything was in my favor. Now I see it from the other guy's position."

When a coach sees a weakness in an opposing corner back, or when a trusted receiver reports that he has the beating of his man, the coach orders the quarterback to persecute the weak link. "Burn him" is the unsentimental instruction.

Even in a team short of real commitment to a bold passing game, Lofton ravages the reputation of most corner backs. In the late summer of 1983 he may well have written the final chapter in the career of a once great corner back, 35-year-old Mel Blount of the Pittsburgh Steelers. The Steelers won in Lambeau Stadium, but Lofton overwhelmed Blount, scoring two touchdowns, one of which left the veteran gasping yards in his wake. Blount at his prime would have attacked Lofton, cracked him in the ribs meaningfully and said, "How do you like those apples, brother?" But in 1983 the zip had gone from Blount. Confronted by a Lofton, he retreated out of fear of getting close and being left for dead by one swivel, one easy change of pace. So he gave Lofton room, and whenever quarterback Lynn Dickey looked up he could see that his number one receiver was free. It was a rare day of luxury for Lofton. He squeezed every yard he could.

Lofton is in the tradition of Stallworth and Swann, which is to say that in the course of a few seconds he can sweep away many deep-seated reservations about the game of football. A big bomb of a pass can illuminate the murkiest of games. There is more to it, of course, than the strong arm of the quarterback and the speed of a Lofton. It is ironic that if the Green Bay Packers had more than a running game occasionally enlivened by the optimism of Eddie Lee Ivery, who plays on despite shattering knee injuries, Lofton's profile would be dramatically higher. The key to a good offense is balance. If a quarterback is confident that he can gain ground by running the ball, he will hand it off to his fullback or halfback without qualms. The opposing defense adjusts to this possibility, linebackers, safeties, corner backs all gearing themselves for a run. It makes them vulnerable to the lofted pass.

Don Coryell, coach of San Diego Chargers, lives by the pass. To increase the balance of his offense, superbly marshaled by the smoky power of quarterback Dan Fouts's right arm, Coryell traded for New Orleans running back Chuck Muncie. It meant that the most formidable attack in the League had been given an even sharper edge. Defensive units go on to the field against San Diego profoundly preoccupied by the prospect of being bombed to oblivion. They are thus wide open to the thrusts of an accomplished running back.

The art of receiving the long pass, the challenge of shaking off "zone" or man-to-man coverage, is now the essence of the NFL game. It is the great spectacle, and it gives the game an extraordinary momentum, especially when the two-minute warning is given to the head coach.

The two-minute warning signals the time for the last push of a team that is losing but is withing striking distance. There are two minutes left to play but not the kind of two minutes that often see a soccer game trickle away with a spate of time-wasting. The NFL cannot permit such anticlimax. The two-minute warning might be described as formal tension. The losing team preserves every second it can, a pass or run being cut off with a swift step over the sideline, which stops the clock. There is something deeply contrived about the two-minute warning, but it generally sets racing the pulses of millions of armchair fans. The two-minute finale, sooner or later, usually involves a prayer. What happens is that the quarterback, perhaps frustrated by a defense willing to grant short gains but guarding against the big play, decides to gamble. He releases the ball in a great spiraling arc, counting on the ability of his selected receiver to outwit or outrun the cover. Then he prays.

It was Knute Rockne who first saw the potential of the forward pass, saw how it could lift the game from the trenches. His ability to find space for himself, his strength and speed, gave Notre Dame quarterback Gus Dorais the opportunity to pick holes in a formidable Army defense. It was fitting that Rockne should have such influence on the way the game would be played down the decades.

FOUR HORSEMEN AND THE GIPPER:
AN IDEA MORE THAN A HERO

Rockne could see both the tactical and the emotional possibilities of football. When he returned to Notre Dame as a coach, he augmented his grasp of the game's technicalities with a fine feel for motivation. He built some wonderfully combative teams, one featuring a unit known as the "Four Horsemen [of the Apocalypse]." He also produced one of the most famous phrases in the history of American sport. He told his team before one game, "Win one for the Gipper."

George Gipp was a former football star of the college. He died before graduation from illness not helped by a wild lifestyle. Rockne presented him as a noble warrior. The facts were somewhat different. There were aspects of George Gipp's personality that were not universally admired, but that mattered little to Rockne or the team. The team won, and many years later an actor named Ronald Reagan would take the part of a highly romanticized Gipp, Pat O'Brien that of Rockne. The film played no small part in popularizing some of the myths of the game.

Don Hutson was not concerned with mythology. He dedicated himself to refining the business of receiving the football at high speed and in dense traffic. Curly Lambeau signed him for the Packers from the University of Alabama in 1935. The great coach described his first glimpse of Hutson as a college player: "He would glide downfield, leaning forward as if to steady himself close to the ground. Then, as suddenly as you gulp or blink an eye, he'd feint one way, go the other, reach up like a dancer, gracefully squeeze the ball and leave the scene of the accident—the accident being the defensive backs who tangled their feet up and fell trying to cover him."

Hutson made the smoothest of transitions from college football to the pros. He could turn crumbs from the quarterback into substantial gains: a bold, clean pass would be converted into a banquet. From his first reception as a professional he scored a touchdown. The Packers had moved the ball 83 yards.

For eight of his eleven seasons in the League Hutson was the top pass receiver, and five times he scored most points. His name is never far from the lips of the veteran fans who go to Lambeau field to wait for James Lofton to warm a wind of withering coldness from off Lake Michigan.

Hutson set standards for those who followed, and for a time there was serious doubt about whether anyone could meet them. Tom Fears and Elroy ("Crazylegs") Hirsch removed the doubt. In the late 1940s and early 1950s Fears and Hirsch offered the kind of joint menace that would, two decades later, be reproduced by Swann and Stallworth. Like many of the best receiver combinations, Fears and Hirsch had different strengths as they provided a dizzying array of options for Los Angeles Rams quarterbacks Norm Van Brocklin and Bob Waterfield.

Hirsch had a genius for the spectacle of the long pass. He executed the effortless gear change of the born runner and had a subliminal sense of time and space. Beside Hirsch, Fears was relatively unspectacular. He lacked his teammate's pure speed, but his brain was as fleet as Hirsch's feet. Together they confirmed Hutson's point. The future of the NFL was about throwing the football.

Today the game bristles with aerial talent. Earlier we discussed the weight of the San Diego passing game, how quarterback Fouts has riches spread before him in the dashing Chandler, the astute Joiner and the perhaps unprecedented Winslow. But, unfortunately for San Diego, their game is seen by many as something of a charade. They are colossal in the air, ramshackle in most other areas, particularly defense. San Diego's challenge is to flesh out the quality of the team. Their passing game should be one of the great forces of American football. It is at present merely an ornament.

There are, as it happens, some far more striking cases of great but isolated talent. Lofton and the bespectacled Jefferson, who used to share receiving duties with Joiner in San Diego before Chandler arrived from New Orleans, are prime examples. Stanley Morgan is another. Morgan performs brilliantly for the mediocre New England Patriots. In Boston Morgan is known as the "Roadrunner." He runs intricate patterns at high speed. Sometimes quarterback Steve Grogan finds the right length and the right pace, but quite often he doesn't. Morgan is left frustrated, another victim of the system that sends the best young players to the worst clubs. Blacks dominate the receivers' ranks almost as completely as whites do the quarterbacking duties. It is a mirror to the black domination of track and field. The job has much to do with explosive speed, a fact conceded by the San Francisco 49ers when they decided to bring in world-class hurdler Renaldo Nehemiah to challenge the aging but still quick Fred Solomon. But then the 49ers also acknowledge that the job can be done without electric speed. Dwight Clark, one of the few whites in the top twenty NFL receivers (Cincinnati's Chris Collingsworth is another) furnishes the evidence.

Clark is a tall, strong man (6 feet 4 inches, 215 pounds) and has excellent antennae for exploring weakness in opposition cover. But he would shrivel in a foot race with such men as Lofton, Chandler and Morgan. What Clark has over most of his rivals is a marvelously dogged streak that carries him into the last minutes of a game with the sharpness he took to the kick-off. He is also extremely disciplined, always where he should be when quarterback Joe Montana releases the ball. It was this discipline that enabled him to average six catches per game over seasons 1981 and 1982 and made him a vital factor in the 1982 Super Bowl at the Pontiac Silverdome, a huge indoor stadium in the suburbs of Detroit. The 49ers overwhelmed the Cincinnati Bengals, one of whose players confessed, "I just couldn't breathe in that place; it seemed so hot, I found myself hyper-ventilating. I guess it was mostly the tension of being out there playing in a Super Bowl."

A former schoolmate said of Clark, "You always knew he would get precisely what he wanted in life. He's a winner from way back." The NFL cherishes such quality and certainly will balance it against the fact that hundreds of young Americans would leap into Clark's shoes and make them move considerably more quickly. But how many of them would have the nerve to run their patterns and time their jumps as the ball flew through the artificial light of a silverdome and all of North America held its breath?

Seattle Seahawks' Steve Largent belongs to the Clark school. Barring a trade to a more powerful club, Largent is unlikely to see Super Bowl action, but the odds are that he will do well. Like Clark, he lacks genuine pace, but he compensates with his calm investigations of defensive frailty.

LARGENT AND CLARK: AN INFUSION OF SUBTLETY

The Largents and the Clarks are perhaps among the great redemptions of football. Take away their guile, their subtle ability to neutralize the extreme athleticism of the men around them, and the temptation would be to dismiss football as not much more than a platform for the fastest and the biggest, for a veritable breed of supermen. Jerry Butler, the Buffalo receiver, had sprint victories over US Olympian Harvey Glance to his credit before he elected to go to his first professional football camp. I once saw the crumpled expression on the face of an extremely able lineman when he was told, "You can play, son, but you're just not big enough." He stood 6 feet 1 inch and weighed 238 pounds. A fine running back caught the eye at one training camp. He stood out with his speed and sure feet and safe hands. But later the coach shook his head and said, "The kid's wasting his time, why, he ain't no bigger than a fob watch." George Best, Sebastian Coe and Pelé might have found work at a football club—as water boys. The Largents and the Clarks fulfill a vital function. They provide evidence that the game is sometimes rewarded for looking beyond the computer printouts of the scouting reports.

Wesley Walker of the New York Jets is another example. He is blind in one eye, a devastating handicap, you might think, for someone whose job demands that he runs at flat-out speed and catches a football which may drop over either shoulder. Walker says, "It's really nothing. It's just that I can't read the eye charts. When I was a kid I used to memorize the big letters."

There are two branches of the receiving business. We have been discussing the wide men, the glamor boys who most often take the catches in the end zone, smash the ball down to the turf and then reach out to the great crowds. Tight ends have their moments in the sun, but at least half their time is spent in the trenches, battling against bigger men. Tight ends both catch and block. They do their catching in the dense skirmishing which goes on down the middle of the field. Blocking duties usually put the tight end against the defensive end, who is invariably huge and startlingly fast, or the middle linebacker, who is the brains of the defense, at least in theory, and tends to build the momentum of an angry rhino. If receivers are the strike planes and the linemen the strategic bombers, the tight end is perhaps the fighter-bomber, quick but also able to produce heavy firepower.

Winslow of San Diego has been called the NFL's quintessential tight end. The 1983 season was his fifth in the League. Each year his reputation grows. One critic not noted for fulsome appraisals wrote, "He blends size and power with the speed, hands and agility of a back. With all the physical tools, Winslow's unique athletic abilities become lethal when mixed with his concentration and intelligence."

No one in the league dominates his position quite as dramatically as Winslow. Some are faster; some are more formidable blockers; but no one has his mixture of delicacy and raw power. The best of the rest is maybe Jimmie Giles of Tampa Bay, who springs from the line with cat-like urgency. He has burning pace and extraordinary resilience. Ozzie Newsome is revered in Cleveland for the poise and imagination that can unlock the most formidable of defenses. *The Complete Handbook of Pro Football* observed in 1980, "Ozzie can make a one-handed catch in full stride look as easy as an anteater snapping out its tongue and collecting an ant for a snack."

Dave Casper of the Minnesota Vikings is the thinking man's tight end. At 6 feet 4 inches and 240 pounds, he is built perfectly

for the job. The bonus is a quick and subtle brain. It won him an
honors degree at Notre Dame and it enables him to steal vital
ground against even the most obdurate of defense. He affects a
country-boy nonchalance but the truth is that he is wound up as
finely as a Swiss watch. Every part works perfectly, a remarkable fact after ten years of rough treatment.

Loften and Chandler, Winslow and Casper are the men who
figure in the most spectacular offenses. They are the other side of
the sword wielded by the quarterback, the cutting edge to the
bludgeoning power of the running game. They get the high
profiles and the high dollars. Yet none of it would work—Lofton
would not fly through the air, Winslow could not surge into open
country, Tony Dorsett would never break free for a huge gain—
if it wasn't for the men of the offensive line. The Hogs. The
grunters and groaners. The guys with the low profiles and,
relatively speaking, the low dollars.

When the Washington Redskins dominated the Miami Dolphins in the 1983 Super Bowl much was made of "Hog-power."
Magazines took color pictures of the huge men of the Redskin
offensive line. The star attraction was usually the aptly named
Russ Grimm, the guard whose ability to yank a 6 feet 6 inch, 280
pound defensive tackle off his feet had given so much momentum
to the stirring deeds of Washington's game winner, running back
John Riggins. The celebrity Riggins was co-opted into
Washington's "Society of Hogs." One suspected it was a brief
vogue. Worse, it seemed that the big men were being patronized
just a little.

The truth is that the dynamics of football insist that the
linemen will labor in obscurity. Their talent is vital to the team,
but the nature of the game is that their performances will always
mean more when the film is run in the coach's room than when
the action unfolds in the stadium. When a Riggins or a Dorsett
breaks free, the crowd cannot really be expected to note the
perfect control of hands and feet with which the offensive line has
sprung open some free ground, or the balance and timing that
has given the quarterback the extra second that allows him to see
that a wide receiver has, in the end, destroyed the corner back.
The great cheers go to the quarterback and the wide receiver as
they return triumphantly to the sideline. What the hogs may get,
a little later, is a pat on the rump from the grateful quarterback
or offensive co-ordinator or perhaps, just perhaps, the head

coach. One suspects that it will always be so; that if the value of the linemen, their integral part in the success or failure of a club is recognized with increasing willingness, their rewards will still follow some way behind.

The best that can be done is perhaps to marvel occasionally at the dedication of these huge men and note that a surprising number of them have the resilience and self-confidence that generate extraordinary staying power and, not least, a sense of their own value in a world somewhat breathlessly given over to the star system. An example of the prejudice against which, say, John Hannah, a superb guard of the New England Patriots, has fought is the old comment of Dick Bestwick, offensive line coach of Georgia Tech. "When you play guard," Bestwick declared, "it's because you're not smart enough to be a quarterback, not fast enough to be a halfback, not rugged enough to be a running back, not big enough to be a tackle and don't have the hands to be an end." Hannah is 6 feet 2 inches tall and weighs 265 pounds. His father Herb played for the New York Giants. John Hannah is generally agreed to be one of the finest guards in the history of the game, perhaps the finest. His feet have a balletic lightness as he protects his quarterback, and there is vast strength as he surges forward against the tackle to create a running block. In the summer of 1983 the 32-year-old Hannah suggested to his New England club that he was weary of the years in the trenches, that he needed to feel there would be some reward for his labors beyond the paycheck and the club's annual failure to penetrate the play-offs. For a time there was an impasse, but no one really doubted that New England would eventually buckle, lure the great man back to their own line or make a trade with one of at least six more powerful clubs who admire Hannah's ability to get the job done.

QUITE A SIMPLE JOB: "KEEP 'EM AWAY FROM JOHN"

There is no doubt that the offensive linemen are entitled to their bouts of liverishness. It was ten years after the dedication of the first building of the Professional Hall of Fame that an exclusively offensive lineman was admitted. A year before Jim Parker was inducted in 1973, the honor went to Texas millionaire and club owner Lamar Hunt. This strange juxtaposition offers an interesting insight into the value system of the National Football League.

Parker got into the Hall of Fame principally for the superb manner in which he protected the great quarterback Johnny Unitas. Baltimore coach Weeb Ewbank, for whom the quarterback was the moon and most of the stars, had told Parker, "Just keep them away from John." Parker followed the instruction zealously, saying, "That was the big rule. If we kept 'em away from John, we ate well." Parker, a native of Georgia, stood 6 feet 3 inches and weighed 275 pounds.

In 1979 Parker was joined in the Hall of Fame by Ron Mix, who in ten years with the San Diego Chargers was penalized for "holding" on just two occasions. The scale of this achievement, what it tells us about the quality of Mix, requires a little explanation. A holding penalty, which costs the offending team 10 yards and can wipe out the most dramatic of touchdown plays, comes when an offensive lineman seeks to win time by clutching a defensive lineman or linebacker. A lineman can hit his opponent with a block, he can restrain with massive forearms, but he cannot attempt to exert a fixed grasp. The challenge is to hold up the progress of a well exercised foe who is applying something like 280 pounds of pressure on your rib cage and do it without hanging on. It is an extremely refined art, as well as being a feat of awesome strength. Mix had wonderfully light feet. He also had a rare talent for an offensive lineman, the knack of getting noticed.

Today the quality of work on the line is unprecedented. Partly it is because of the relentless growth of coaching; partly it is the relentless growth of the players themselves. Mike Wilson of Cincinnati is one of the best of the current offensive tackles. He stands 6 feet 5 inches and weighs 275 pounds. He is as assertive as he should be. At the other end of the Cincinnati offensive line there is the equally commanding presence of Tony Munoz, a brilliantly acute player who survived three knee operations during this career at the University of Southern California. It is no coincidence that the Cincinnati quarterback Ken Anderson completed successfully 70 per cent of his passes in the 1982 season. Munoz and Wilson give Anderson a sense of deep well being when he steps back into the pocket before releasing the ball. Keeping the quarterback healthy is a basic requirement. Keeping him tranquil is a wonderful bonus.

Mention of such men as Munoz and Wilson, Mike Kenn of the Atlanta Falcons, Marvin Powell of New York Jets, Cody Risien of Cleveland Browns and Matt Herkenhoff of Kansas City is rare when the big plays explode across the television screens. Nor is much made of the work of centers like Webster of Pittsburgh (it has been said that he resembles the meanest truck driver in the world), Dwight Stephenson of Miami and Pete Brock of New England. One respected critic says of Brock, "Brock likes his nose tackles with toast and orange juice."

Sometimes you sense that the offensive linemen enjoy their martyr's crown; that amid all that immense power there is a hint or two of masochism, though it is for obvious reasons an unconfirmed speculation. One coach says, "I guess you need a certain mentality to play the offensive line. Maybe it's better if you are a little bit introverted, if you're someone who likes to do a job well, and knowing that you've done well is enough. You don't need the band to play everytime you accomplish something."

Perhaps all the lineman asks is that when a James Lofton or a Wes Chandler climbs into the bright light and takes the catch, a few observers will cast their minds back through the flow of the action, remember how it was that the quarterback, his feet fluttering like a nervous matador, had the time to wait for a Lofton or a Chandler to win his space. Hopefully, some observers will recall that the line stood in the face of the charge, cool and implacable, pre-empting the danger of a penalty flag being thrown to the ground. With luck, one of those observers will be the man who signs the paychecks.

10

The Destroyers

B utkus. Lambert, Reynolds. Klecko. Youngblood. Matuszak, Sturdy names, are they not? It is as well. We are not talking quarterbacks here. We are not discussing the beautiful flight of the football, the Hollywood profile of Vince Ferragamo or the Arabian thoroughbreds of Joe Montana or how Terry Bradshaw's marriage with former ice-skating champion Jo Jo Starbuck is progressing. We are not talking about the prima donna receivers and their balletic leaps. We are talking defense. Or, as thousands of voices roar it in Cincinnati's Riverfront Stadium or Pittsburgh's Three Rivers, D-E-F-E-N-S-E. . .

Offense is the shop window of football. Defense is the heart and the conscience and, often, the entrails. Ultimately, the offensive unit will settle the game—though occasionally the knock-out is delivered by the withering impact of an interception and touchdown run—but the defense will establish its standard.

The master defender is the linebacker. He has to have speed and strength and a biting sense of time and space. The middle linebacker is the captain of defense. Ideally, he draws an intellectual pleasure from destruction. Dick Butkus was possibly the greatest middle linebacker of all time, though it is a claim not to be aired in the company of Jack Lambert and Jack "Hacksaw" Reynolds.

In his *Thinking Man's Guide to Football* Paul Zimmerman quotes Butkus's old teammate Mike Ditka thus: "With the highest respect I've got to say Dick is an animal. He works himself up to such a competitive pitch that on the day of the game he won't answer a direct question. He'll grunt."

Chicago Bears took Butkus from the University of Illinois as their first-round draft pick in 1965. Until 1973 he subjected the NFL to something close to a systematic reign of terror. His hitting was so hard that his name became synonymous with the violence of the game. Once the team bus of a team retreating to the airport was struck by a car. One of the players said, straight-faced, "It's Butkus." Halas, coach and owner of the Bears, was entranced when he first saw Butkus playing for the university. He advised him to trim down to 245 pounds for the sake of mobility. Halas wanted more than a phenomenal hitter. He wanted someone to control his defense. Butkus complied, and throughout his professional career his weight never wavered from the 245-pound mark.

Butkus told Zimmerman, "Every time I play a game, I want to play it like it was my last one. I could get hurt and that would be it for keeps. I wouldn't want my last game to be a lousy one. Some people think I have to get down on all fours to eat my couple of pounds of raw meat every day. Others think that George Halas taught me to walk upright and that I have an agent to do my reading and writing for me. But people who really know me know that I can read a little. I move my lips sometimes but I can read things on a second-grade level—like newspapers. I don't need a rubber stamp to give an autograph."

There, in those cryptic comments, you have much of the linebacking spirit. It is as though the linebacker embraces the extremes of this violent game, is obsessed with an investigation of human fortitude. In his nine years of professional football Butkus created much physical havoc, both among his opponents and for himself. His post-football days have never been free from nagging pain, a residual of collisions that looked, and sometimes sounded, like freeway disputes between runaway trucks.

The football historian George Sullivan once cited the time when a gathering of NFL scouts was asked to name the man they would most confidently send behind enemy lines to assassinate a leader. Each scout nominated a linebacker. They were paying tribute to the men who fill what is arguably the game's most demanding position, and they were also perhaps defining the qualities required of an able assassin. Sullivan wrote, "You have to know precisely when you should hold your ground, drift back, or charge in. And once it's time to make a move, you have to make it with authority, with brutality even."

The linebacker has to hit runners and blockers when his opponents attack along the ground; he has to read the keys of the offense to protect against a pass. And he has to answer the call "Red Dog" when the coach makes a full-blooded commitment to sack the quarterback. It is the football equivalent of a commando raid. Success is rewarded with a stunning blow to the morale of the offensive team. But the "blitzing" maneuver carries risk. The quarterback, if he is cool enough, quick enough, has the potential for a swiftly flipped pass into an area denuded of defenders. The blitz has to operate at maximum speed; indecision is disaster. The term "Red Dog" goes back to 1949, when Catfish Cody, a forerunner of Butkus with the Chicago Bears, sacked his quarterback thirteen times. Cody was said to have looked like a mad dog. "Red Dog" was the code for an all-out blitz from the three linebackers.

San Diego's quarterback Fouts has described, perhaps not altogether whimsically, how he anticipates a blitz. "Sometimes you can see it on the faces of the linebackers," said Fouts. "Their eyes bulge. Sometimes you sense they're going to foam at the mouth."

Jack Lambert crossed these pages earlier and inevitably. If Chuck Noll, creator of the Pittsburgh dynasty, had to start all over again, the first player he would probably choose is Lambert. The Pittsburgh Steelers are the NFL's lunchbucket team, a team whose followers work in the steel mills and down the coal shafts of Pennsylvania. These followers may cheer the artistry of a Lynn Swann, the poise of a Terry Bradshaw, but most of them would admit that deep down they go to Three Rivers Stadium on days crackling cold to celebrate the spirit of Jack Lambert. He has been described as "Godzilla the middle linebacker," and before the 1983 season the 31-year-old won this assessment from one critic: "He's an animal at the point, an obsessed pursuer and a human radar station tracking down receivers." One of the side effects of Lambert's physical prowess—he is 6 feet 4 inches tall and weighs a modest 220 pounds—is that many of the local steelworkers fantasize about their ability to take him on. This fantasy becomes most compelling when Lambert pops into a bar for a beer or two, and on several occasions he has been obliged to separate a man from his dreams.

Technically, Jack "Hacksaw" Reynolds has never been in the class of a Butkus or a Lambert or, certainly, the great Ray Nitschke of the Green Bay Packers. But Reynolds, who at 36 was on the fringe of the San Francisco 49er plans at the start of the 1983 season, has surely created for himself an enduring place in the folklore of linebacking.

Reynolds's passion for the game, and specifically his passion for winning, was established in his unversity days in Kentucky.

He was thrown into such anguish by one defeat that he proceeded to saw his jeep in half. He required thirteen hacksaws. He completed the job, grim-faced. His willingness to research opponents is something of a legend. He has his own film room at home and has been known to spend whole nights there, absorbing the patterns of play favored by upcoming opponents. He moved from Los Angeles Rams to San Francisco in the ebbing days of his career, and some thought the 49ers' coach Bill Walsh was making a backward step, was investing more in a reputation than in a player. But Walsh was proved right when Reynolds exerted a huge influence over the 49ers as they swept to their 1982 Super Bowl win. "We got more than a player when Jack Reynolds came here," said Walsh. "We got a lot of emotion. We got an idea."

Joe Klecko is senior member of the New York Sack Exchange. The Sack Exchange is the popular name for the defensive front four of the New York Jets. The other members are Mark Gastineau, who has the habit of dancing over fallen quarterbacks, Abdul Salaam and Marty Lyons. If Reynolds is, emotionally speaking at least, the definitive linebacker, Klecko is perhaps the prototype defensive end or tackle. He is a former truck driver from Pennsylvania. His specialty is a powerful surge toward the quarterback. There are more subtle linemen, men more alert to the "draw" or the "trap" of an offensive line eager to lure the destroyers into a vacuum. Klecko missed most of the 1982 season. Before the 1983 season he announced that he was functioning perfectly once more. He had been refitted.

Klecko, who is 30, winces when Gastineau does his victory dance. It offends his sense of decent behavior. Crushing a quarterback to the turf, at least hitting him hard enough to "ring his bell," is an obligation; indeed, the sensation is the great reward of the job. Nick Hebeler, a defensive end in the Canadian Football League, explains. "This may sound strange, but making a quarterback sack is, for me, perfection. I go to training camp and get into shape. I work hard through the week, gearing my mind and my body to fulfilling my assignments. I take tremendous punishment through the game, so much that for several days after a game I can't move properly. And all the time you have this driving force. You want to get to the quarterback. You want to hit him, you want to punish the other team. It keeps you going. And then it happens. The feeling is, well, sublime."

After he said that he grinned, a little sheepishly. "That's heavy stuff to be talking about a football game. But while you're doing it, it's your life. You stick out for better contracts and things like that because you know it's a short life and when it's over you will have to go back into the real world. And every time you go on to the field you know you can get injured, quite badly. But deep down you know that you'd probably be doing it for nothing."

Jack Youngblood of the Los Angeles Rams played in the 1980 Super Bowl against medical advice.

Contrary to all expectations, the Rams came close to toppling the Steelers. Most of the praise for this moral triumph went to the precocious performance of young quarterback Ferragamo, who threw four touchdown passes and caused the Pittsburgh defense embarrassments they had not known for the best part of four years. But within the dressing-room many players pointed to Youngblood as the chief source of their inspiration. A quick, powerful defensive end, Youngblood had performed in the play-off games with a broken bone in his lower leg. Every sudden movement brought deep pain. After the defeat of Tampa Bay, Youngblood could not stand up. It was another example of what is loosely described as the spirit of defense.

The spirit of John Matuszak is perhaps a little less easily defined. Certainly it is wild, a conclusion reached by the Californian Highway Patrol one night when they stopped Matuszak's car and discovered a Magnum revolver and a machete. Matuszak's line of work was intimidation. In this he was much helped by his physical appearance. He stood 6 feet 8 inches tall and weighed 275 pounds. He once told the host of a late-night TV talk show that his idea of a pleasant evening was to take a bottle of vodka to a hot tub in the company of three "nice ladies." He then roared with laughter, some of it, you sensed, self-mockery. Matuszak retired in 1982, leaving a vast hole in the Los Angeles Raiders' defensive line. During preparations for the 1981 Super Bowl in New Orleans, in which he played a vital part in the defeat of Philadelphia Eagles, Matuszak joined some friends in the French quarter. He got involved in what was later described as a "serious party." He was fined, but his place in the team was never really in jeopardy. Matuszak devoured runners.

The presence of a Matuszak carried football close to a moral question of some delicacy, one that asked about the legitimate boundaries of violence in any sport. In the opinion of many, the tactics of Jack Tatum carried the game way beyond those borders.

Tatum played free safety for the Oakland Raiders for nine years. In the assessment of his club, they were nine extremely productive years. A free safety's job is to patrol the last line of defense, sweep forward on running plays, seek out and destroy receivers in passing situations. It is a job that requires pure speed. Tatum covered 100 yards in even time. It also requires brutal strength. Tatum has an upper body of oak tree proportions.

In 1979 Tatum published his autobiography. Its title was *They Call Me Assassin*. Tatum wrote: "My idea of a good hit is when the victim wakes up on the sidelines with train whistles blowing in his head. I like to believe that my best hits border on felonious assult."

Two of America's most influential sports writers were appalled. Jim Murray of the *Los Angeles Times* wrote: "It's frightening, it casts doubt on a whole way of life and it indicts a national institution . . . a casebook study on the destruction of a young athlete by a cruel system." Jerry Izenberg of the *New York Post* said, "If professional football is really about some of the things he says it is, then maybe those of us who really enjoy the game had better ask ourselves who we are and what we are about."

In his nine years with Oakland Tatum acquired a fierce reputation for heavy hitting and also a tendency to aim late, "cheap" shots at unguarded opponents. Once Rocky Blier, a Vietnam war veteran and a respected running back with the Pittsburgh Steelers, wrote a letter to the League protesting Tatum's tactics. The Pittsburgh coach Chuck Noll, angry about a Tatum shot that left wide receiver Lynn Swann with a concussion, charged that "criminal elements" were operating in professional football.

Had Tatum merely argued that he was engaged in a tough, ruthless business and that physical accidents were bound to happen in a game so committed to heavy body contact, there would probably have been no great furore. But he was perceived to be isolating and glorifying the violence . . . and celebrating his own part in it.

Then there was the quite sickening affair of Darryl Stingley.

Stingley was a wide receiver for the New England Patriots, a lithe, sleek runner. I once met him on a visit to Muhammad Ali's training camp in the Poconos Hills, west of Philadelphia. He said what a pleasure it was to meet the great Ali, who had done so much for his people. He was a quiet, courteous man who, when I met him, had very sad eyes. He was sitting in a wheelchair.

Tatum recounts the Stingley incident. "August 12, 1978, I was involved in a terrible accident with Darryl Stingley. On a typical passing play, Darryl ran a rather dangerous pattern across the middle of our zone defense. It was one of those pass plays where I could not possibly have intercepted, so because of what the owners expect of me when they give me my paycheck, I automatically reacted to the situation by going for an intimidating hit. It was a fairly good hit, but nothing exceptional, and I got up and started back toward our huddle. But Darryl didn't get up and walk away from the collision. That particular play was the end of Darryl Stingley's career in the NFL. His neck was broken in two places and there was serious damage to his spinal cord.

"Darryl Stingley will never run a pass pattern in the NFL again, and it may be that he will never stand up again and walk across a room. For weeks Darryl lay paralyzed in a hospital and there were times when I wondered about myself and the structure of the rules."

Shortly before the Stingley incident, Tatum had been involved in contract talks with Oakland owner Al Davis. Tatum recalled those talks. "Al was telling me that I was paid to be a war head and anyone who came near me should be knocked to hell. Al left me with the impression that my only marketable talents in professional football were those of an intimidator. My job with the Raiders was that of a paid assassin. Well, so be it."

For a while there was much public revulsion over the Stingley affair, and it resurfaced with the publication of the Tatum autobiography, which some perceived to be no more than callous exploitation of the tragedy. Others, however skeptical about the motivations for publication, agreed that the book did turn a light on some of the murkier aspects of America's game. Tatum was one of the League's most notorious "hitters," a man whose mere presence on the field concentrated the minds of receivers dramatically. But the question was one of degree. Upon every defensive player there is an obligation to hit, to punish. There are moments of fine skill, when a bomb of a pass is tipped from the grasp of a receiver or when a passing play is read so well that the interception is made cleanly and with the opposition end zone 30 or 40 yards of clear field away. But these are the rare bonuses for the men of defense. The fundamentals are the sack, the savage moment of triumph and the crunching collisions that sometimes seem to shake the very foundations of a great stadium.

Glen Jackson, a fine outside linebacker in the Canadian League, allows that there is a certain madness to his job. "I'm coming up to 30 years old, and I know that one of these days a coach is going to tap me on the shoulder and say, 'Jackson, you're finished.' And what will I have when it's over? I'll have a busted-up body and a degree in geography. What the hell am I going to do with a degree in geography? My wife sees me crawling around the house for a couple of days after a game. She says, 'Haven't you had enough? When will you have had enough?' I tell her I don't know, but really it's a lie. I'll never get enough of that feeling you get just before a game. I can't really describe it. For me, there is no other feeling like it. You hear the crowd in your ears when you run on the field and then, when the game is on, it's just a buzz. There is just you and the guy you've got to get to, got to hit, and then if you make the hit, you get this tremendous feeling of peace, of well being. The day after the game your body really starts to hurt. But you don't forget how it felt when you hit the guy, when you made the play."

Jackson and the great Butkus always knew the certainty of physical discomfort. These days Butkus can scarcely walk. Jackson says he might get a job selling after he has made his last hit. The other certainty is that for Butkus and Jackson, for Hacksaw Reynolds and Joe Klecko, and for up-and-coming destroyers like George Cumby of Green Bay and Clayton Weishuhn of New England, the violence of football will always remain the most compelling of drugs. The NFL is rightly serene about the fact that the gridiron trenches will always be filled.

11

A Brutal Trial

I t starts with training camp. This is where a football club is forged. This is where the coaches set stop watches and take notes, look on with cold eyes as the young men run into each other. Endlessly the coaches take notes and run cameras. It has been said that football is not a contact sport but a collision sport. In training camp they watch carefully how well the players collide and how swiftly they get up when the collision is over. Training camp is pitiless. Sometimes a kid does not make it through the front door. Paul Brown, the celebrated coach of Cleveland Browns, once noticed that a hopeful young player had arrived in crumpled jeans and scuffed sneakers. He ordered the player to seek out the club's transport manager, who would make arrangements for his journey home. It was a long way.

An NFL training camp lasts six weeks. More than 100 players are pared down to a final roster of forty-eight. In recent years this harsh selection process has received some cosmetic attention, but football is a brutal game, and the only way you can truly test a candidate is to inflict some measure of brutality.

Before the main camp there is a free agents' training camp. A wide net gathers in a variety of fish. Most are either minnows or dreamers. For several years Rube Berry, a slow-talking Oklahoman who is currently coach of the Saskatchewan Roughriders in the CFL, was in charge of recruitment for the British Columbia Lions. The Canadian League was then the first option of players who failed to establish themselves with NFL clubs. Now the Canadians have to compete with the infant USFL for the NFL leftovers.

Berry recalled how it was when a young American, rejected by the big League, automatically turned his thoughts to Canada. "The mail was unbelievable. It is a little scary to think about how many young guys out there dream of making it as football players. Some of the letters had to be checked out. A guy will give his college, his time over 40 yards, his physical dimensions and you think, 'Well, maybe this guy slipped through the net.

Maybe he could make it.' But mostly you scratch out a brief reply and toss the letter into the trash can.

"I got letters from taxi drivers, from guys working in car plants. They all have the same story. They just haven't had a chance. I even had a letter once from a one-legged guy. He thought he could overcome his handicap. He believed in himself, you know?"

Training camps are still designed to strip self-belief from all but the very strong, the men who can make it through to the League. But nowadays only a few of the coaches persist openly with the old style of management. The pills are sugared. The "hazing" of "rookies," which used to be an elaborate and sometimes physically dangerous practice, now usually involves the young player standing up to sing a song while veteran players heckle and throw bread rolls. In the old days there was more of Flashman, the bully of *Tom Brown's Schooldays*.

The bullying was certainly more overt. It flowed down from the head coach. "Lombardi was fair," said the players, "he treated us all the same—like dogs. . . ." Joe Paopao, a quarterback from Los Angeles, admits that there have been times when he has sat in his room in training camp and wept for all the broken dreams around him. "You work out with the guys every day, you eat your meals together, you drag yourselves to your rooms, dog-tired, and then the next morning they're gone. Rubbed out. And you know how much they wanted to make the team. In a way, it's like losing brothers."

It is a brotherhood that gathers from every corner of American life. There are huge, ruddy-faced sons of farmers from the Midwest. There are black, lean fliers from the South. There are tall, blond quarterbacks from California. They meld in their pursuit of this great American dream of "making the club."

Whatever the style of management, the tension rises inexorably. It has to do with the reality of the situation, which is that initially there are at least three or four players for every vacancy. You sit across the lunch table from a man who has your own background, your own ambitions and who, if you talk to him long enough or deeply enough, may turn out to be an extremely pleasant guy. But usually such conversations are avoided because in a half-hour you may have to hit this man so hard that ideally he will cease to have any stomach for his ambitions. You do this because he is maybe the only thing between you and the bright lights of the National Football League.

Across the field there are a series of dramas. There is the "pit," where the linemen appraise each other and then charge, like vast, muscular stags. Pairs of them wrestle in a line, grunting and sweating in the sun, and along the line walk the coaches. Sometimes the coaches frown when one of the linemen is too easily thrust aside by his antagonist. Sometimes the coaches take a note of such a lapse, and if the lineman is aware that this has happened, he may mumble some excuse about lost footing or laugh incredulously, as though some rare disaster has befallen him. It is unusual for the note to be erased.

The quarterbacks stand in batteries, showing off the power of their throwing arms as receivers blaze along their routes and as back-stepping cornerbacks dog them in search of the flashy interception that might inspire a shout of approval from the coach. Once I saw this happen and the cornerback did a back-flip in his jubilation. As I remember, he didn't make the club.

The kickers fire mortar shells at the posts. They are moved back 5 yards after every successful attempt. The elimination process is as relentless as any on this field of groaning effort. Many of the kickers appear comic beside the behemoths. Here you may see a roly-poly pastry cook from Austria, pressed into his uniform and aiming for a place in the American game. Kickers tend to be oddballs. John Smith, an English school-teacher and part-time soccer player from Gloucestershire, made it with the New England Patriots.

Smith walked into his American dream in 1973. He was attending a summer camp as a soccer instructor. One day a basketball coach from New York watched him idly kicking the football. The coach said that he would talk to some football people he knew. The Patriots gave Smith a trial, then traded him to the Pittsburgh Steelers, who allowed him to drift into the limbo of sandlot football. But Smith was dogged, and he tried again with the Patriots. He battled through the ordeal of free agents' camp and became a fixture at New England's Boston stadium. In 1979 he was the League's most successful kicker, landing twenty-three field goals from thirty-three attempts. In 1982 he was the center of controversy when the Patriots drove a snowplough on to the field and cleared a patch for Smith to kick a winning field goal against the Miami Dolphins.

Now Smith lives in a luxurious home on Cape Cod. He says, "Looking back, it is extraordinary. If the basketball ball coach hadn't seen me larking around with the football, if I'd lost my nerve in the training camp. . . . Some people think kickers are separate from the game, that they just march on and have a poke at the ball, then march off. Well, it's not as simple as that. You spend most of the games in those huge stadiums waiting for a chance to do something. Then often you get in a situation where you know your contribution is going to be vital. You feel the pressure building. I suppose that's what training camp is all about. I mean, seeing how you cope with pressure."

Sometimes the pressure in the training camps is lifted bizarrely. Alex Karras, a wild, gambling lineman of the Detroit Lions, once hired a private airplane to buzz his club's practice field. He had the pilot bombard the players and coaches with green jockstraps.

Tom Brown, a superb middle linebacker for the British Columbia Lions, arrived in Canada via Minnesota and the US Navy, with which he served in the China Sea off Vietnam and learned how to drink copious amounts of beer. Brown broke the tension at the Lions' training camp by vowing that he could stay longest on the bed of the river that flowed through the little town of Courtenay on Vancouver Island. Brown marched into the river carrying a boulder above his head. Players and towns-people moved along the river bank in pace with the boulder. They swore Brown was submerged for three minutes.

In the old days it was common for platoons of coaches to watch over the players at night. Strict curfews were imposed. Today there is more sophistication. A player has to prove himself at the morning and afternoon sessions, in the full-scale "scrimmages" and, if he survives the early-morning taps on the doors of those players who have failed, the exhibition games that lead into the regular season. Players tend not to break training-camp curfew these days. Mostly they are too exhausted from the physical work and the long sessions poring over playbooks and looking at film. Those who still have energy left tend to weigh the cost of a night on the town against the prospect of a high salary and the glory of being involved in the big game.

The NFL publicity department suggests that there are few more dazzling prospects across the whole spectrum of American life. Certainly, the great stars, the Namaths and the Bradshaws, the O. J. Simpsons and the Joe Montanas, enjoy a rich harvest. But down in the "Pit," in the special teams and among those players who scuffle on the edge of the big team, training camp is too often the door to disillusionment. For every player who knows the exhilaration of stepping out beneath the bright lights and the drawing of a big paycheck, there are dozens who feel used, who leave the game knowing that most of their hopes were romantic.

Ironically, the long and acrid strike that devastated the 1982 season is likely to result only in the worsening of such tensions. Though NFL salaries are generous by the standards of most legal employment, they are greatly inferior to those of baseball and basketball, and many feel that the collective bargaining agreement that ended the strike will shorten the careers of established players. The new agreement demands bonuses for long service. The reaction of the owners of the twenty-eight clubs, who have almost always operated as a united front against any hint of "socialism" or true freedom of contract, is expected to be the brisk lopping off of many veterans. The already brief average career length of an NFL player—4.5 years—will inevitably be further reduced.

COUNTING THE MILLIONS . . .
AND GIVING TICKETS TO RIDE

In 1983 Kevin Lamb of the *Chicago Sun-Times* reported: "The sharp increase in veterans' minimum salaries under the National Football League's new collective bargaining agreement could price as many as a dozen [Chicago] Bears out of the League in the next year or two. The most vulnerable Bear is a twelfth-year veteran, Bob Parsons. He is trying to negotiate downward from the $150,000 base salary the Bears were required to offer him.

"The new minimums will require substantial base salary increases of more than 15 per cent for six other non-starters: a linebacker, Bruce Herron; two defensive backs, Doug Plank and Walt Williams; a kicker, Bob Thomas; a tackle, Don Jiggetts; and a tight end, Brooks Williams. The base salary of another linebacker Jerry Muckensturm, will increase 11 per cent, though he seldom played over the last two years because of a shoulder injury.

"Throughout the League, the new wage scale figures to affect enough players that agents and general managers are talking ominously about an influx of younger and cheaper players."

Jim Finks, general manager of the Bears, told Lamb, "If you had a player on your team who had been somewhat of a contributor for four or five years but not a first-stringer, and you look at the chart and see now you've got to pay him $30,000 more than you paid him last year, I think you've got to take a look at yourself."

Finks's use of language is interesting: "If you had a player on your team who had been somewhat of a contributor. . . ." For "somewhat of a contributor" we might read Jerry Muckensturm, the linebacker with the banged-up shoulder. We might think of his getting $30,000 a year more as some kind of extraordinary largesse. But then we should consider some other matters. We should think of how each year billions of dollars are waged on the outcome of NFL games; of how millions of dollars' worth of television advertising is scooped in every time a player goes down injured or a coach calls a time-out. Of how each club draws in more than $13 million from the television networks before a ticket is sold or a cent is made from a can of beer or a hot dog or a tub of popcorn.

We should think of the gentle, bewildered face of Darryl Stingley as he waved goodbye to Muhammad Ali and his helpers carefully placed him in the back of the ambulance. And of Joe Paopao, the "throwin' Samoan", who wept for his brothers when the coach knocked on their doors at dawn and handed them air tickets. Air tickets to where? Who knows. We should think of old Hacksaw Reynolds and his dogged dreams, of Dick Vermeil talking about burn-out with the tears rolling down his cheeks, of Mrs. Lombardi getting a public dressing-down from the great Vince and of Norm Van Brocklin pulling off his jacket and offering to fight the world.

The game is really as Joe Kapp, the brawling, drinking anarchist quarterback of Berkeley, the BC Lions and the Minnesota Vikings, said it was. It is more than a game. It is America, good and bad, tough and sentimental, dynamic and gaudy. It is the All-American war game, and it is also apple pie and a big brassy band. It is brute strength and endless ingenuity. It is pain and glory and arrogance and an intense need to prove yourself. Yes, Kapp was right. Football may indeed spread to foreign fields. But it could only have happened in America.

General Glossary

AUDIBLE	Also known as a check-off. When a quarterback wishes to change a called play at the line of scrimmage, he informs his teammates by calling an audible. These plays are usually called when the quarterback "reads" or spots an unexpected defensive alignment.
BLITZ	When a defensive team puts pressure on the quarterback by rushing with a player who is not normally used as a pass rusher. The most common blitz involves the use of a linebacker (also known as a "Red Dog") or a defensive back ("safety blitz").
DOWN	One play in a series of four downs. A team must gain 10 yards in a series of four downs to retain possession of the football with another series of four downs. The downs are numbered sequentially: first down, second down, third down and fourth down.
FIELD GOAL	A scoring play in which a player kicks the ball over the crossbar of the goal post between the two uprights. The kick is usually a placement in which a player takes a snap from the center and then holds it upright for the kicker. The rules also allow for a drop-kick, in which the kicker bounces the ball on the playing surface and then kicks it, but this technique is no longer employed. A field goal is worth 3 points.
FREE KICK	After surrendering a safety, the team that is scored upon kicks off to the defensive team. This kick is known as a free kick and is a punt, in which the defensive team is not permitted to rush the kicker.

FUMBLE

When a team player loses control of the football and drops it. The ball is free and any player can recover it.

GOALPOST

Located on the goal line, the goalpost consists of one center topped by a crossbar and two poles called uprights on either end of the crossbar. The goalposts are employed on field goal and point-after kicks, and a successful kick must clear the crossbar and pass between the uprights.

HANG TIME

The amount of time a kick remains in the air. Teams attempt to improve on the hang time of a kick because it gives the kick-coverage team time to go downfield and tackle the kick returner.

HUDDLE

A gathering of the players before the ball is scrimmaged. In the offensive huddle the quarterback calls the play and gives his team the snap count, the signal on which the center will snap the ball to begin the play. In the defensive huddle one player, usually the middle linebacker, calls for a defensive formation.

INTERCEPTION

When a defensive player catches a pass thrown by the offense.

KICK-OFF

At the beginning of each half and following each score, the play is begun with a kick-off. The kicking team at the beginning of the game and at the start of the second half is determined by a coin toss. After a field goal or a touchdown, the kicking team is the team that has scored.

LATERAL PASS OR LATERAL

A pass or a toss to a player who is stationed behind the passer. This type of pass may be made at any point on the field, and the ball is free if it is not caught.

POINT AFTER TOUCHDOWN

After scoring a touchdown, a team is permitted to attempt to earn a bonus point by kicking the ball through the uprights, as in a field goal, or by running or passing the ball into the end zone from the 5-yard line.

Kicking is the most common way of scoring the extra point.

POST PATTERN

A pass pattern in which the receiver runs straight down the field.

PREVENT DEFENSE

A prevent defense is generally used in the final minutes of the half. The defense is designed to keep the offensive team from completing a long gain. The defense surrenders short passing patterns and running plays but strengthens its efforts against long plays.

PUNT

A kick, usually on fourth down, in which one team surrenders possession of the ball to the other team. The punter takes a direct snap from the center and then kicks the ball without allowing it to touch the ground.

RECEPTION

When an eligible player successfully catches the ball cleanly in bounds.

SACK

When the quarterback is tackled behind the line of scrimmage before he is able to throw a pass.

SAFETY TOUCH

A scoring play in which an offensive player is forced back into the end zone and is tackled. A safety touch is worth 2 points.

SIGNAL

Commands from the quarterback before the start of a play. The quarterback signals can be used to change a play (see AUDIBLE) and are used to notify the players when the ball will be snapped.

SNAP

The exchange of the ball from the center to begin a play. The most common snap involves the center handing the ball through his legs to the quarterback. The center can also snap the ball with a long pass through his legs to the quarterback, to another back or to a kick holder or punter.

SPECIAL TEAMS

Players employed in kicking situations. They are usually younger reserve players or players with special talents, such as kick returners or players with open-field tackling skills.

SPOTTER | A coach, usually an assistant, who watches the game from the press box and relays information to the bench through a telephone hook-up.

SWEEP | A running play to the outside.

TACKLE | A defensive move in which a ball carrier is brought to the crowd, thus ending a play.

TOUCHBACK | When the ball lands in the end zone on a punt or a kick-off, the receiving team can elect not to attempt a runback and take a touchback. In this case the ball is moved out to the 20-yard line. A touchback can also be taken following an interception and is automatic in cases where a kick goes through the end zone.

TOUCHDOWN | A scoring play in which the ball is moved across the opponent's goal line, either by a run or by a pass. A touchdown is worth 6 points.

TWO-MINUTE DRILL | Also known as a hurry-up offense. A series of plays employed in the final minutes of a half. In this offense the premium is on moving the ball into scoring position in the least amount of time. Time-saving devices include passes out of bounds to stop the clock and the calling of several plays at one time, eliminating the need for a huddle between plays.

TURNOVER | A play that results in the defensive team obtaining possession of the football. Interceptions, fumble recoveries and a failure to gain 10 yards in four downs fall into this category.

Glossary of Penalties

CLIPPING A block from the rear: 15-yard penalty.

HEAD SLAP When a defensive player slaps an opposing lineman on the helmet: 15-yard penalty.

HOLDING Infraction in which an offensive player uses his hands to hold or impede the progress of a defensive player. There is also defensive holding in which the defender prevents a player from running a pass route or moving to a loose football: 10-yard penalty.

ILLEGAL CHUCK A defensive player is allowed to make contact with a pass receiver once, but he must do so before the ball is thrown and while the receiver is within 5 yards of the line of scrimmage. Any other contact constitutes an illegal chuck and a 10-yard penalty.

ILLEGAL PROCEDURE A 5-yard penalty is assessed for a number of procedural mistakes on the part of the offensive team. Procedure penalties are assessed when a team does not have at least seven men on the line of scrimmage, when a back moves forward before the ball is snapped or when a play crosses the line of scrimmage before the ball is snapped.

INTENTIONAL GROUNDING When a quarterback deliberately throws an incomplete pass to avoid being tackled for a loss. The ball is declared dead at the point where it was thrown.

OFFSIDE When a player crosses the line of scrimmage before the ball is snapped: 5-yard penalty.

PASS INTERFERENCE When a player makes contact to prevent an opponent from catching the ball. The offensive and defensive players are both entitled to catch the ball, and interference can be called against either side. Defensive interference, the most common penalty, results in an automatic first down at the point of infraction. Offensive interference results in a 15-yard penalty.

PILING ON

Also called a late hit, this roughing penalty is assessed when a player jumps on a player after a whistle has been blown to end a play, or hits a player after he has gone out of bounds. The penalty is 15 yards and an automatic first down.

ROUGHING

There is a variety of roughing penalties that call for a 15-yard penalty and an automatic first down. Infractions include kicking, grabbing an opponent's face mask and contact after a whistle has been blown or when out of bounds.

ROUGHING THE PASSER

A 15-yard penalty and an automatic first down are awarded if a defensive player tackles the quarterback after he has completed his throwing motion.

ROUGHING THE KICKER

Defensive players are not permitted to make contact with the kicker while he is kicking the ball. The exception is when the defensive player blocks a kick and his momentum carries him into the kicker: 15-yard penalty and automatic first down.

SPEARING

When a player uses his helmet to hit a player on a tackle or a block: 15-yard penalty.

TIME-COUNT VIOLATION

Also known as taking too long in the huddle. A 5-yard penalty is assessed against a team that fails to put the ball into play within thirty seconds.

TOO MANY MEN

A 10-yard penalty is assessed when a team has more than eleven men on the playing field.

UNSPORTSMANLIKE CONDUCT

This penalty covers a range of infractions from talking back to an official to fighting. Penalty is usually 15 yards, but flagrant fouls, such as fighting, can result in a 25-yard penalty and ejection from the game.

Glossary of Positions

CENTER
An offensive lineman responsible for putting the football into play by snapping it to a player in the backfield, usually the quarterback. This player is so designated because he lines up in the middle of the offensive line.

CORNERBACK
A defensive back who lines up on the outside of the defensive formation and provides coverage on the wide receivers. These players are prized for their speed and quickness.

DEFENSIVE ENDS
The primary pass rushers in the defensive formation, these players line up at either end of the defensive line, usually opposite the offensive tackles. The position requires a combination of strength and quickness; the player must be big and strong enough to fight off the block of an offensive tackle and quick enough to chase a quarterback or a running back. In addition to rushing the passer, the defensive end has a responsibility to "contain" an offensive play by keeping the opposition backs from running wide and forcing them back into the middle of the playing field.

DEFENSIVE TACKLE
These are the behemoths of the defensive line. Their main responsibility is to seal off the middle on running plays and to provide support for the ends in rushing the passer. Many teams have switched from a four-man line to a three-man alignment. In this formation there is only one tackle, and he is referred to as a NOSE TACKLE, MIDDLE GUARD or NOSE GUARD.

GUARD
An offensive lineman who is aligned on either side of the tackle. In addition to the usual responsibilities of pass-blocking and straight-ahead blocking on running plays, guards are sometimes required to "pull out" and lead the blocking around the end on sweeps.

LINEBACKER
These are probably the most athletic players on the defensive unit. They are required to provide coverage against the run and are also an integral part of the pass defense, usually covering the tight end or a running back coming out of the backfield. In a conventional 4–3 defense there are two outside linebackers and one middle linebacker, while a 3–4 defense employs two outside and two inside linebackers. Inside linebackers are usually bigger because they must defend against power running inside, while outside linebackers are generally quicker because they must cover outside plays going wide to the sidelines. The middle linebacker is usually regarded as the defensive quarterback because he normally calls the defensive signals.

PUNTER
The kicker who kicks the ball in punting situations, usually on fourth down. The punter lines up behind the center and takes a direct snap, then strikes the ball with his foot without allowing it to touch the ground. Distance is important in assessing a punter's performance, but teams also place a great emphasis on "hang time," the length of time the ball remains in the air. The longer the hang time, the more time the kick-coverage team has to get downfield to tackle the kick returner.

QUARTERBACK
The central player on offense. The quarterback takes the snap from center on most offensive plays and attempts to move the ball forward by handing the ball to a

running back throwing the ball to an eligible receiver or by running with the ball himself. The quarterback also calls the plays, deciding what play to run either by himself or with the help of a message from his coach.

RUNNING BACKS
This is the designation applied to most offensive backs in pro football, although some teams still refer to them as FULLBACKS and HALFBACKS or TAILBACKS. Classic fullbacks tend to be larger and are known as power runners, while halfbacks tend to be smaller and quicker.

SAFETY
An inside defensive back, the safety is responsible for providing pass defense of opposing backs and for helping the cornerbacks to cover wide receivers.

TACKLE
An offensive lineman who lines up at either end of the five-man interior line formation. Tackles provide pass-blocking coverage against defensive ends and also provide straight-ahead blocking for running plays. Tackles are larger than guards and are seldom required to block downfield. On running plays their main responsibility is to open an initial hole for a running back.

TIGHT END
An eligible pass receiver, the tight end is usually employed on short-pass patterns, generally across the middle. Tight ends are usually much larger than wide receivers and are not as fast. Tight ends are also used as blockers on running plays, and many teams use a second tight end in place of a wide receiver on plays when the team needs only a short gain for a touchdown or a first down.

WIDE RECEIVERS
The principal target on long passing plays. Wide receivers line up on the offensive flanks, and their main responsibility is to run a pass pattern and attempt to find an opening in the defense. Speed is the prime

asset for a wide receiver, although some players at this position have compensated for a lack of speed either with their catching ability or with their ability to find openings by means of feints or other moves.

Index

Numbers in italic refer to the diagrams; numbers in bold to the plates.